Scoring High

Iowa Tests of Basic Skills®
A Test Prep Program for ITBS

Book
6

SRA

A Division of The McGraw-Hill Companies

Columbus, Ohio

www.sra4kids.com

SRA/McGraw-Hill

A Division of The **McGraw·Hill** *Companies*

Send all inquiries to:
SRA/McGraw-Hill
8787 Orion Place
Columbus, OH 43240-4027

Printed in the United States of America.

ISBN 0-07-572819-2

4 5 6 7 8 9 QPD 09 08 07 06 05

On Your Way to Scoring High
On the Iowa Tests of Basic Skills®

Book 6

Name _____

Vocabulary

Lesson 1a **Vocabulary**

Directions: Read the phrase and the answer choices. Choose the answer that means the same as the underlined word.

Sample A	A good <u>income</u>		Sample B	A <u>vital</u> activity
A	A amount owed		**B**	J needless
	B bargain			K necessary
	C investment			L pleasant
	D money earned			M harmful

- • Look at each answer choice carefully.
- • Try substituting each answer choice for the underlined word. This will help you find the right answer.

1 An <u>enormous</u> tree
A old
B huge
C beautiful
D oddly-shaped

2 To <u>persist</u> for years
J resist
K continue
L study
M follow

3 <u>Sufficient</u> for now
A too much
B too little
C enough
D unnecessary

4 To <u>deny</u> him permission
J allow
K give
L offer
M refuse

5 <u>Link</u> the ideas
A separate
B join
C identify
D like

6 Cross the <u>channel</u>
J narrow waterway
K wide road
L hot desert
M mountain pass

7 A strong <u>guarantee</u>
A desire to join
B group of friends
C business
D promise of quality

8 <u>Reveal</u> the truth
J carefully hide
K make known
L look for
M disbelieve

GO ➡

9 **Approach** a town
- A recognize
- B live in
- C go away from
- D come near to

10 **Irritate** people
- J annoy
- K help
- L enjoy
- M visit

11 A **forceful** person
- A weak
- B foreign
- C strong
- D helpful

12 A **direct** answer
- J honest and truthful
- K dishonest and untruthful
- L correct
- M incorrect

13 A successful **venture**
- A athletic competition
- B business
- C risky activity
- D career

14 To **convince** someone
- J fool
- K anger
- L persuade
- M be familiar with

15 The **insistent** sales person
- A talented
- B not very capable
- C friendly
- D not giving up

16 A **blunt** answer
- J correct
- K difficult
- L long and detailed
- M short and rude

17 **Ordinary** people
- A unusual
- B normal
- C kind
- D surprising

18 **Shred** paper
- J fold carefully
- K make by hand
- L cut into strips
- M throw away

19 Feel **relieved**
- A satisfied with
- B without worry
- C angry about
- D slightly sick

20 A **significant** discovery
- J profitable
- K surprising
- L unexpected
- M important

STOP

Vocabulary

Lesson 1b **Vocabulary**

Directions: Read the phrase and the answer choices. Choose the answer that means the same as the underlined word.

Sample A	**A long conflict**	
	A	friendship
	B	time
	C	project
	D	struggle

Sample B	**Migrate with many others**	
	J	move
	K	return
	L	disagree
	M	build

• **Skim the items. Look for words you know. Answer those items first.**

1 Much wisdom
A   knowledge and good judgment
B   ability to play sports
C   kindness and wanting to help
D   feeling that someone is smart

2 Attend a meeting
J   be late for
K   leave early from
L   be present at
M   arrive early at

3 Delay her trip
A   enjoy
B   pay for
C   dislike
D   put off

4 A slender branch
J   thick
K   thin
L   strong
M   weak

5 Be cautious
A   friendly
B   calm
C   careful
D   happy

6 Similar clothes
J   different
K   expensive
L   dull
M   alike

7 A large structure
A   mountain
B   window
C   building
D   vehicle

8 Unusual weather
J   not normal
K   not pleasant
L   bad
M   good

STOP

Answer rows   A Ⓐ Ⓑ Ⓒ Ⓓ   1 Ⓐ Ⓑ Ⓒ Ⓓ   3 Ⓐ Ⓑ Ⓒ Ⓓ   5 Ⓐ Ⓑ Ⓒ Ⓓ   7 Ⓐ Ⓑ Ⓒ Ⓓ
                B Ⓙ Ⓚ Ⓛ Ⓜ   2 Ⓙ Ⓚ Ⓛ Ⓜ   4 Ⓙ Ⓚ Ⓛ Ⓜ   6 Ⓙ Ⓚ Ⓛ Ⓜ   8 Ⓙ Ⓚ Ⓛ Ⓜ

Test Yourself: Vocabulary

Unit 1

Directions: Read the phrase and the answer choices. Choose the answer that means the same as the underlined word.

Sample A In this <u>section</u>
A home
B newspaper
C auditorium
D part

Sample B Make a <u>pledge</u>
J promise
K profit
L process
M provision

1 <u>Dodge</u> the other players
A confuse
B defeat
C avoid
D cheer

2 An old <u>basin</u>
J kitchen cabinet
K bowl for water
L box for food
M cooking tool

3 Discuss the <u>situation</u>
A length of time
B state of affairs
C recent news
D type of weather

4 A <u>major</u> problem
J recent
K simple
L small
M large

5 The <u>distant</u> mountains
A near
B high
C far
D tall

6 A full <u>pantry</u>
J clothes closet
K food closet
L large pot
M wooden box

7 <u>Jagged</u> rocks
A sharp
B heavy
C moss-covered
D multi-colored

8 To <u>launch</u> the business
J enjoy
K visit
L manage
M begin

GO

4 **Answer rows** A Ⓐ Ⓑ Ⓒ Ⓓ 1 Ⓐ Ⓑ Ⓒ Ⓓ 3 Ⓐ Ⓑ Ⓒ Ⓓ 5 Ⓐ Ⓑ Ⓒ Ⓓ 7 Ⓐ Ⓑ Ⓒ Ⓓ
                 B Ⓙ Ⓚ Ⓛ Ⓜ 2 Ⓙ Ⓚ Ⓛ Ⓜ 4 Ⓙ Ⓚ Ⓛ Ⓜ 6 Ⓙ Ⓚ Ⓛ Ⓜ 8 Ⓙ Ⓚ Ⓛ Ⓜ

9 To seem <u>petrified</u>

A confused
B frightened
C hungry
D exhausted

10 Fix the <u>wound</u>

J injury
K clock
L broken pipe
M ripped cloth

11 A <u>lean</u> runner

A fast
B thin
C tired
D injured

12 Understand the <u>manual</u>

J road sign
K collection of poetry
L book of instructions
M television guide

13 A <u>concealed</u> door

A locked
B heavy
C hidden
D swinging

14 She liked the <u>bouquet</u>.

J wedding gift
K kind of dress
L picture frame
M bunch of flowers

15 To <u>view</u> the paintings

A look at
B create
C enjoy
D talk about

16 The <u>coarse</u> cloth

J colorful
K rough
L shiny
M striped

17 Nothing but <u>nonsense</u>

A hopeless attitude
B worthless money
C meaningless talk
D careless actions

18 An <u>abrupt</u> stop

J sudden
K slow
L planned
M difficult

STOP

Directions: Read the passage and the answer choices. Choose the answer you think is better than the others.

Sample A

As the car pulled out of the driveway, Lamar took one last look at the house he had lived in for ten years. He and his family were moving to a new house near the beach in Florida. It was a wonderful house, and his new school was going to be fabulous. Even so, looking at his old house gave Lamar a lump in his throat.

How did Lamar probably feel about moving?
A   Mostly happy
B   Mostly sad
C   Worried and angry
D   Happy and sad

- **Skim the passage quickly, but don't try to memorize it. Refer back to the passage to answer the questions.**
- **Look for key words in the question and answer choices. They will help you find the right answer in the passage.**

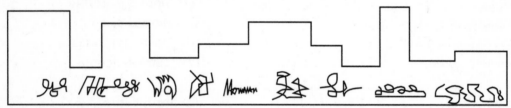

"Is that you, Enrique?" called Mr. Torres from his big chair in front of the television.

"Yeah, it's me, Dad," answered Enrique as he shut the front door behind him.

"Come in here a minute, son, I want to talk to you," said Mr. Torres.

Enrique sighed and slowly walked toward his father with his hands in his pockets. "I really need to do something in my room, Dad."

"Listen, Enrique. Isn't it a little late for you to be coming home from Lloyd Carlson's house? I know it's a Friday night, and there is no school tomorrow, but I don't like you out on the streets at this hour."

"Hey, Dad, the Carlsons just live in the next block. It's not like I've been walking all over town," replied Enrique, gesturing with his hands.

"What's that on your hands, son?" asked Mr. Torres. Enrique looked at his hands and saw streaks of blue paint. "Oh, Lloyd and I were working on some models. I guess I wasn't very careful with the paint."

"Okay, Enrique, off to bed. We'll talk about this more tomorrow. I don't want you out on the streets when it gets this late, even if it's just a block away. Things happen." Mr. Torres turned off the television and sat in his chair thinking about his son. He sighed, then he went out to the garage to see if the door was closed before

GO

he went to bed. He noticed that the can of blue spray paint was not on the shelf where it belonged.

The next morning, Mr. Torres called the Carlsons on the telephone. When he finished speaking to Mrs. Carlson, he hung up the phone and sat drinking a cup of coffee until Enrique came into the kitchen for breakfast.

"Well, good morning, son," said Mr. Torres with a smile. "You and Lloyd are in for a big surprise next Saturday. There's a very special event taking place in town, and the Carlsons and I have signed you two boys up."

Enrique's face lit up. "What is it, Dad? A Bike-a-thon? A basketball game? Is a celebrity coming to town?"

"No, son," said Mr. Torres. "None of those things. It's our city's third annual Paint the Town Day. About a thousand people are getting together to paint over graffiti that has been spray painted on walls, fences, and buildings. The only celebrity you're likely to see is the mayor, who is handing out 5,000 gallons of paint and brushes for this project."

Enrique's face fell. "You know, huh?"

"Yes, Enrique. Lloyd's parents thought you boys were over here last night. When I told them I thought you were over there, we figured out what you had done. My first impulse was to call the police, but Mr. Carlson suggested we give you one more chance. On the phone this morning we came up with this idea as a suitable way for you boys to pay the community back for what you have done," said his father. "Graffiti makes our city look bad and costs a lot of money to clean up. So next Saturday, you and Lloyd are going to put in a long day's work."

"Okay, Dad. It was a stupid thing to do, and I'm really sorry. Lloyd and I never did anything like that before, and I promise we won't do it again. Next Saturday, we'll be the two best painters. You can count on it."

1 How did Mr. Torres feel when he noticed the can of blue spray paint was gone?
A Suspicious
B Relieved
C Angry
D Sad

2 Paint the Town day is an example of
J a way to punish young people who have done bad things.
K a way to celebrate the founding of the town.
L an opportunity for people to paint their houses with the town"s paint.
M a community project to make the town a better place to live.

3 In this story, what is a "fitting punishment?"
A One that is easy for the boys to do
B One that fits the boys' plans
C One that suits the crime
D One that is difficult for the boys to do

4 What do Mr. Torres and the Carlsons hope to do with their plan?
J Teach Enrique and Lloyd to be responsible for what they have done.
K Make the boys angry because they have been caught.
L Help the boys understand the importance of coming home on time.
M Make the boys stay home at night and do their homework.

5 Why does Mr. Torres worry about Enrique?
A His school grades are getting lower.
B He often gets in trouble with Lloyd.
C Bad things can happen late at night.
D The boys need their sleep.

It was a cold, rainy afternoon. Mary Lou and her grandmother were in the attic of her grandmother's Iowa farmhouse entertaining themselves by looking through the contents of a battered old trunk.

"These old clothes are a riot, Grandma. Did people really wear things like this?" asked Mary Lou.

"They certainly did," replied Grandma. "Your aunts and uncles wore them and thought themselves elegant, indeed."

Mary Lou laughed and pulled an old candy box out of the trunk. She lifted the lid and found a packet of letters tied with string. "These letters look really old, Grandma. See how the envelopes are tattered and yellowed. You couldn't mail a letter today with a one cent stamp on it."

"Who wrote them?" asked Mary Lou, trying to read the flowing, graceful handwriting.

"Well, they are addressed to my mother and father, and the postmark shows they were mailed from Neversink, New York," Grandma noted as she flipped through the envelopes in the packet. "They are all from my father's mother whose name was Anna Thomas." Grandma removed the string from around the letters. She carefully opened an envelope and removed the letter.

"The writing is very fancy," commented Mary Lou.

"Telephones weren't available in Iowa until after 1900. If Anna Thomas wanted to stay in touch with her son and his wife who had moved from New York to Iowa, she had to do so by writing letters. Penmanship was very important, and people took pride in showing a fine hand," said Grandma.

"What does the letter say?" asked Mary Lou.

Grandma adjusted her eyeglasses and read:

Dear Children,

I think you must have had a hard time building your house. When I read the newspapers and they told about the snow storms, I could not sleep nights to think how hard you must have it. Jeanie, I was glad you sent me a lock of your hair. I will send you a lock of mine and wish you would send a lock of Arthur's. I will send you some of my lettuce seed. You must have the plants about a foot apart and hoe it like you would cabbage. Write soon and have faith. There is trouble everywhere, and you will overcome yours.

Your loving mother,
Anna

When Grandma finished reading, Mary Lou was quiet for a moment and then whispered, "I think she must have missed them a lot and worried about them because they were so far away from her."

"Yes, I'm sure she did. Anna never saw her children again, you know. But she wrote them almost every week, and they wrote back to her. Even though they were more than a thousand miles apart, they remained very close." Grandma looked at Mary Lou and put her arm around her. "We are fortunate to have these letters, Mary Lou. Someday when you have children, I hope you will read the letters to them. Nothing would please me more than to know my grandchildren had the opportunity to learn about my grandmother's life."

GO

6 **What made Mary Lou think the letters were old?**
J   They were in the trunk.
K   The stamps were strange.
L   They had pictures with them.
M   The way they looked.

7 **The postmark on an envelope shows**
A   from where the letter was mailed.
B   who wrote it.
C   where the letter is going.
D   who will receive it.

8 **Why were Mary Lou and her grandmother going through the trunk?**
J   They like the attic.
K   The electricity was out.
L   There was not much else to do.
M   It was too hot outside.

9 **In this story, "showing a fine hand" means**
A   having good penmanship.
B   having nice hands.
C   dressing with nice gloves.
D   writing often to friends.

10 **What surprised Mary Lou?**
J   Where the letters came from
K   The way people dressed long ago
L   That her grandmother wanted to go to the attic with her
M   That people wrote to each other rather than using the telephone

11 **Who wrote the letters Mary Lou found in the old trunk?**
A   Mary Lou's mother
B   The mother and father of Grandma
C   The mother of Grandma's father
D   Mary Lou's grandmother

12 **What does the word "elegant" mean in the third paragraph?**
J   Very unusual
K   Funny
L   Without many colors
M   Showing good taste*

13 **In the letter Anna Thomas wrote to her family in Iowa, she said she could not sleep nights because**
A   she had read about the snowstorm in the newspaper.
B   she wanted a lock of her son's hair.
C   she wanted Jeanie to grow lettuce from the seeds she sent.
D   there was trouble everywhere.

14 **At the end of the story, Grandma expresses her belief that**
J   Mary Lou should write letters to her very often.
K   she missed her children who lived far away.
L   children should learn about their family's history.
M   letters are the best way to learn about family members.

STOP

Reading Comprehension

Lesson 2b **Reading Comprehension**

Directions: Read the passage and the answer choice. Choose the answer you think is better than the others.

Sample A   The Denner family solved a problem in an interesting way. They tired of mowing their lawn, watering it, and using chemicals on it. One day, they decided to take out their lawn and replace it with a wildflower garden. Their beautiful, carefree garden has become the talk of the neighborhood.

Why is the wildflower garden the talk of the neighborhood?

A   People talk about things they don't understand.

B   The neighbors don't like it.

C   People must think it is a wonderful idea.

D   The flowers are cut and put in vases.

- **Sometimes the answer is not stated in the passage. You have to "read between the lines."**

Directions: As part of a pen pal project, Ashihiro kept a journal of what the weather was like on the first day of every month for his friend in Argentina. Use the journal to answer questions 1–6.

March 1   This is probably the most miserable day of the year. It's raining, cloudy, and the wind is blowing. When we have weather like this on the weekend, my computer gets a good workout.

April 1   It snowed almost 10 inches last night! Only kidding … it's an April Fool's Day joke. Today is beautiful, and my friends and I are going to the park to play baseball. I play the outfield and am pretty good, but not as good as my older sister.

May 1   The wind is really blowing and a storm is coming in. The weather report says we might have thunder and lightning for the first time this year. I love storms, as long as I can be inside.

June 1   School will be over in two more weeks! I hope the weather is like this all summer. The temperature is supposed to be 70° and there isn't a cloud in the sky.

July1   What a dreadful day! The tempeture is already 80°, and it's damp and sticky. I wish we had a swimming pool, but living in the city in an apartment makes that impossible.

August 1   The weather has finally started to cool off. All of July was humid, almost exactly like the day I wrote you. I couldn't sleep at night because it was so sticky. I hope it stays cool for a while.

September 1   School starts in four days. If the weather then is as miserable as it is today, I might not even go. Actually, I love the first day of school because I get to see everyone and it's so busy we don't have much work.

October 1 The fall colors have been spectacular, and today is a perfect day to enjoy them. The sky is blue, there are just a few clouds, and the sun is bright. I feel sorry for people who don't have trees that change color in the fall.

November 1 Winter is definitely here. It's cold, gray, and in general, nasty. The temperature is still in the 20's, and I'm not looking forward to school at all. I have to walk to school, and I hate getting there wet.

December 1 When December rolls around, everyone in school starts thinking about the holidays. This year, everyone is thinking about the weather. We have had the snowiest winter in history. It's like living in Alaska. Two feet of snow fell last night, and there was already a foot on the ground. Pretty soon, we'll have to dig tunnels to get around.

1 **What can you conclude about where the writer of this journal lives?**
A It is usually warm.
B It is usually cold.
C It has good weather.
D It has four seasons.

2 **How do the journal entries change from March to September?**
J They focus less on the weather than on the writer's feelings.
K They become much shorter.
L They talk more about the writer's family.
M They focus more on the weather than on the writer's feelings.

3 **What was the weather in July like?**
A Cooler than usual
B Hot and sticky without a breeze
C It rained more often than usual.
D The wind made the weather nasty.

4 **How does the writer feel about the first day of school?**
J Bored about school
K Excited to go
L Sad that summer is over
M Happy to go to a new school

5 **What does the writer mean in the March first entry when he says "his computer will get a good workout"?**
A He will work hard to earn money to buy a computer.
B He will go to the gym before using his computer.
C He will spend the day using the computer.
D He will exercise instead of using his computer.

6 **In the entry for September, what does the word *miserable* mean?**
J Pleasant
K Unusual
L Usual
M Unpleasant

GO

High expectations were a part of life in the Alvarez household. Dr. Walter Alvarez sometimes sat in his reading chair for an entire evening. He was not snoozing—far from it. He was using this time to think of new problems to solve. This had an impact on young Luis Alvarez.

Luis's father had left a medical practice in San Francisco to join the staff at the Mayo Clinic in Minnesota. Luis was not terribly interested in his father's work, but he did inherit a feverishly curious mind. The clinic was one of the world's largest medical centers, and Luis found the labs there fascinating. His high school summer vacations were soon spent apprenticing in the clinic's instruments shop.

Luis enrolled at the University of Chicago and took a few chemistry classes. Physics—the science that deals with matter, energy, motion, and force—became his passion. One of Luis's professors had won a Nobel Prize in physics. Luis made it a point to read every word this man had ever written. Luis was totally dedicated. By 1936, he had earned his bachelor's, master's, and doctor's degrees.

Luis was then invited to join the University of California Berkeley Radiation Lab. True to form, Luis spent about a year reading everything ever been written about nuclear physics. He also got to know the lab inside and out. Luis would often disappear into the library there and reemerge days later. His eyes would be bright and his mind bursting with new ideas and solutions. Like his father, he was always pushing himself to be the best and to discover new things. He found it surprising if others did not challenge themselves in a similar manner.

During World War II, Luis was head of Special Systems at MIT. The radar research lab was affectionately nicknamed Luis's Gadgets. There, Luis developed a ground controlled approach technology or GCA. It allowed ordinary aircraft to land at night or in times of poor visibility with the help of an observer on the ground. He also spent time at the Los Alamos nuclear research lab. Still later, his work with cosmic rays would give him the idea of x-raying an Egyptian pyramid. This procedure helped determine whether there were hidden chambers within.

During Luis's lifetime, he received numerous awards for his wide-ranging scientific work, including the Nobel prize in physics. Despite these awards, he is most well known for the theory he and his son, Walter, developed about the extinction of dinosaurs. They found evidence to suggest that an asteroid struck the earth, raising so much dust in the atmosphere that it changed the climate enough to cause the extinction of many plants and animals.

GO

7 **In what way did Walter Alvarez have high expectations?**

A He demanded a lot from his son, Luis.

B He wanted to be the highest paid physician.

C He expected people to do things for him.

D He was always pushing himself to be the best.

8 **How did Luis Alvarez feel about his father's work?**

J Inspired and challenged to outdo it

K Somewhat uninterested by it

L Eager to understand it better

M Disappointed that it brought few awards

9 **In the fourth paragraph, what is the meaning of *true to form*?**

A To be honest about something

B To put your trust in something

C To do something that you've done before

D To try something new

10 **Why would Luis Alvarez's new concept for landing aircraft be called "ground controlled approach"?**

J Aircraft were guided by an observer on the ground.

K Aircraft needed special equipment on board to land.

L Aircraft were required to see the ground before landing.

M Aircraft used radar instead of sight to locate the ground.

11 **Based on the information in the passage, Luis Alvarez's legacy of invention and discovery live on. What does this mean?**

A His children have gone on to become scientists.

B His ideas and concepts are still being used.

C His appetite for reading has inspired other readers.

D His difficult life stands as an example to many.

12 **This passage presents Luis Alvarez as**

J a great scientific mind.

K a gifted physics instructor.

L someone who has little patience for people who give up easily.

M someone whose research got less recognition than it deserved.

13 **What is this passage mainly about?**

A Luis Alvarez's relationship with his father

B A brief overview of Luis Alvarez and his career

C Important scientific developments after World War II

D The importance of learning as much as you possibly can

STOP

Answer rows   **7** Ⓐ Ⓑ Ⓒ Ⓓ   **9** Ⓐ Ⓑ Ⓒ Ⓓ   **11** Ⓐ Ⓑ Ⓒ Ⓓ   **13** Ⓐ Ⓑ Ⓒ Ⓓ   **13**

                 8 Ⓙ Ⓚ Ⓛ Ⓜ   **10** Ⓙ Ⓚ Ⓛ Ⓜ   **12** Ⓙ Ⓚ Ⓛ Ⓜ

Directions: Read the passage and the answer choices. Choose the answer you think is better than the others.

Sample A An unusual Presidential election took place in 1789. It was the first election in U.S. history, and George Washington ran without opposition and was chosen unanimously by the electors from each state. Ironically, Washington almost refused to run!

What is the meaning of the word *unanimously* in this passage?
A   By most electors
B   By a few electors
C   By all electors
D   By exactly half the electors

Letterboxing is an interesting combination of treasure hunting, navigation, and exploration. It began when someone long ago left a calling card in a bottle in the countryside of Dartmoor, England.

A letterboxing event begins with someone hiding a watertight box in a beautiful, interesting, or remote location. Inside the box are a logbook or journal and a carved rubber stamp. The person who hides the box writes the directions or "clues" for locating the buried treasure. The clues can be simple and direct or complicated and puzzling. They often include a map and landmarks that will help you find your way.

With a set of clues in hand, the letterboxer tries to find the box. A seasoned letterboxer carries a pencil, a rubber stamp, an inkpad, and a logbook. When the buried box is found, several things take place. The letterboxer marks the once-hidden logbook with his or her personal stamp. This logbook serves as a record of who has successfully found the letterbox. The letterboxer then stamps his or her personal logbook with the rubber stamp from the box. Personal logbooks are a letterboxer's bounty. They keep track of a letterboxer's many conquests.

How do you get started? Most important, you need clues. Dartmoor's letterbox clues are published in a catalog. In the United States, letterboxing is just catching on. You have to go to the Letterboxing North America Web site at www.letterboxing.org. True letterboxers say the most exciting clues are learned by word of mouth. It's also fun to find clues to a new site inside a box you've just found.

As the sport of letterboxing spreads, it is important to be respectful of the environment. Wherever clues may lead, you must remember to leave the place as you found it. Read your clues carefully. Most of them tell you exactly where to dig or to look and will help you avoid damaging the area.

1   Which of these is the last thing a person who is hiding a letterbox does?
A   Write directions on how to find the letterbox.
B   Put a logbook and a stamp in the letterbox.
C   Select a remote location to hide the letterbox.
D   Leave a personal calling card inside the letterbox.

GO

2 **According to the passage, the most exciting clues are**

J published in a catalog.

K found on the Internet.

L spread by word of mouth.

M found inside letterboxes.

3 **Why are there clue catalogs in England but not in the United States?**

A Letterboxers in England prefer catalogs to Web sites.

B Letterboxing is something you pay for in England.

C Letterboxers in the United States like a challenge.

D Letterboxing has just begun in the United States.

4 **How has the author organized this passage?**

J By describing how basic letterboxing is done

K By listing each item needed for letterboxing

L By comparing English and North American letterboxing

M By explaining in detail the history of letterboxing

5 **Which of these best summarizes the author's view of letterboxing?**

A It is a great way to meet people who love the outdoors.

B It is an interesting hobby that threatens the environment.

C It is a fascinating and exciting modern-day treasure hunt.

D It is an ancient practice that is best left in England.

6 **According to the passage, what is the purpose of a hidden letterbox's logbook?**

J Recording one letterboxer's discoveries

K Keeping track of who has found the box

L Providing searchers with misleading clues

M Making sure letterboxers keep the location a secret

GO

The animal world has some very strange characters. Consider the opossum, an animal that makes its home in North America. About 20 inches long and weighing about 15 pounds, the opossum is a marsupial, which means it carries its young in a pouch on the abdomen. What's more, the opossum has more than 50 teeth and can open its mouth extremely wide, more than 90°. When threatened by enemies, the opossum just rolls over and plays dead, hoping the predator will leave it alone.

Another marsupial is the kangaroo, a native of Australia and New Zealand. It has huge hind legs, a muscular tail, and small front legs. It spends much of the time upright, standing on two legs and leaning against its tail. With its strong legs, a kangaroo can leap more than 30 feet and travel at more than 30 miles an hour.

The anteater is a toothless animal that eats—you guessed it—ants. Found from Mexico to Argentina, anteaters have powerful claws that can tear open the nests of ants and termites. With its long snout and even longer tongue, the anteater quickly makes short work of its victims. What is hard to believe is that an animal that eats ants can grow to fifty pounds and measure about six feet from snout to tail.

In the northern ocean swims a member of the whale family that has a horn on its head. One of the teeth of the narwhal—it only has two—grows out of its upper jaw and develops into a twisted tusk that can be over nine feet long. The narwhal apparently uses this tusk to stun fish, squid, and other small sea creatures, which it then eats. During the Middle Ages, the tusk of the narwhal gave rise to the legend of the unicorn.

Not many animals are a threat to the deadly cobra, but the mongoose certainly is. This small animal looks something like a mink and is around twenty inches long with a fifteen inch tail. It is incredibly fast and clever, and when it is matched against a cobra, it almost always wins. People believe that the mongoose is not affected by cobra venom, but it is the thick fur of the mongoose that prevents the snake's teeth from sinking in.

7 **The poison a cobra injects when it bites an animal is**
- A fast and clever.
- B incredible.
- C ineffective.
- D called venom.

8 **What does it mean to *play possum*?**
- J Show your teeth
- K Pretend you are dead
- L Climb up a tree quickly
- M Leave predators alone

9 **It is reasonable to conclude that anteaters**
- A came to SouthAmerica from Africa.
- B eat just a few ants.
- C have many sharp teeth.
- D eat lots of ants.

10 **What is the author's purpose in writing this passage?**
- J To show that animals that live in different places are often similar
- K To describe how strange animals can be amusing
- L To explain how animals have been misunderstood in the past
- M To entertain and inform the reader by describing some strange animals

11 **How are opossums and kangaroos alike?**
- J They both have unusual teeth.
- K They are about the same size.
- L They are both marsupials.
- M They are both good climbers.

GO

Stuffed animals and dolls are among the most popular toys ever created. Years ago, these toys were handmade for a child from scraps of material by a parent, relative, or friend. They were so loved by the young recipients that toy companies took over the market. Today, most stuffed toys are made by large companies, but they are still enjoyed by millions of children and a surprising number of adults.

Stuffed dolls and animals that are modeled after characters in familiar story books are especially popular. Winnie-the-Pooh and his friends Piglet, Heffalump, Kanga, Roo, and Eeyore have all been copied in fabric. *The Velveteen Rabbit* is a book written about a small boy's special affection for a stuffed rabbit and the rabbit's wish to become real. After the book was published and became successful, velveteen rabbits had to be manufactured to meet the demand created by the book. Even cartoon and television characters like Charley Brown and his dog, Snoopy, have ended up in fabric.

Probably the most popular stuffed toy has been the teddy bear. In 1903, a newspaper cartoon showed President Theodore Roosevelt refusing to shoot a young bear while on a hunt. A Brooklyn, New York, toy store owner, Morris Michtom, made a small brown bear of plush material with shoe-button eyes. The cub was named Teddy in honor of Roosevelt, and millions of teddy bears have been manufactured or homemade since.

12 **Why are so many storybook characters made into stuffed animals?**
J It's hard to think of a good stuffed animal character.
K Young children like stuffed animals they know from storybooks.
L Storybooks are not very expensive.
M You can read and hold a stuffed animal at the same time.

13 **Which word best describes most tuffed toys?**
A Exciting
B Comforting
C Expensive
D Stiff

14 **What is the main topic of this passage?**
J How toys imitate characters
K The origin of stuffed toys
L How stuffed toys are made
M A popular and cuddly toy

15 **How were the first stuffed toys different from those you buy today?**
A They were made for children by friends and family members.
B They were made of soft fabric.
C Children loved them very much.
D They were more expensive because of the materials that were used.

GO

One of the hit movies of 1995 was *Little Women,* a story about life in New England in the middle of the nineteenth century. What makes this movie unusual is that the book on which it is based was written by Louisa May Alcott in 1868. For a story to have such great appeal a century after it was written is a tribute to the writer's ability to reach her audience.

Alcott was born in 1832 in Germantown, a small community just outside of Philadelphia. Her family was never in very good financial condition because her father, a well-known educator, was constantly involved in strange schemes that always lost money. Louisa, her three sisters, and her mother believed in their father, however, and their hard life brought the family members closer together.

All of the girls worked to help the family make ends meet. Louisa May was a seamstress, servant, and school teacher before she turned to writing. She sold her first story in 1852 and followed that success with a number of others. Alcott wrote thrillers, fairy tales, and magazine articles which helped her build a good reputation and earn a decent living.

During the Civil War, Alcott served as a nurse and wrote often to her family. Her letters were later compiled into a book published under the title *Hospital Sketches,* which built her reputation further. Another novel, *Moods,* followed, and after traveling to Europe, Alcott returned to America and published *Little Women.*

In many respects, *Little Women* seems to be autobiographical. It describes the March family and their struggle to make ends meet during hard times. The four girls in the story—Jo, Meg, Beth, and Amy—are much like Louisa May and her sisters, and the difficulties faced by the March family in the story are remarkably similar to those of the Alcott family.

Little Women was a huge success and made Louisa May Alcott both rich and famous. Her earnings from the book allowed the family to move to a comfortable home in Massachusetts where Alcott became friends with many noted writers. She published several other successful novels before her death in 1888 and is recognized today as one of America's finest writers.

16 **How does the author portray Louisa May Alcott in this passage?**
J   As a writer who always enjoyed life because she was successful
K   As a writer whose books were meant for young children
L   As a successful writer who ended up in poverty
M   As a talented writer who loved her family

17 **In the second paragraph, what does the word "schemes" mean?**
A   Plans
B   Jobs
C   Groups
D   Enemies

18 **Why is *Little Women* felt to be autobiographical?**
J   The family in the book lived over a century ago.
K   The family in the book had children.
L   The family in the book was much like Alcott's family.
M   The family in the book lived in a large house.

STOP

Spelling

Lesson 3a **Spelling**

Unit 3

Directions: Fill in the space for any word that has a spelling mistake. If there is no mistake, fill in the last answer space.

Sample A	A	prevail
	B	happyest
	C	sacrifice
	D	laughter
	E	(No mistakes)

Sample B	J	opposite
	K	evaporate
	L	base
	M	postage
	N	(No mistakes)

- **Remember, you are looking for the word that has a spelling mistake.**
- **If you are not sure which answer to choose, take your best guess.**

1
A plain
B thrifty
C comfortable
D beach
E (No mistakes)

2
J carnuval
K patch
L lifetime
M failure
N (No mistakes)

3
A move
B endure
C claw
D marshall
E (No mistakes)

4
J spring
K editting
L industrial
M wonderful
N (No mistakes)

5
A muffle
B frontier
C soler
D appeal
E (No mistakes)

6
J guessed
K acquire
L opposite
M documint
N (No mistakes)

7
A influence
B prohibit
C semester
D baloon
E (No mistakes)

8
J principle
K pour
L hoarse
M interfere
N (No mistakes)

GO ➡

9
A chapter
B neglect
C peresh
D earn
E (No mistakes)

10
J lead
K diploma
L rare
M kindnes
N (No mistakes)

11
A signature
B marjin
C comics
D creak
E (No mistakes)

12
J release
K sujjestion
L bound
M coward
N (No mistakes)

13
A subtract
B radio
C napkin
D continint
E (No mistakes)

14
J stretch
K assistance
L effect
M origin
N (No mistakes)

15
A coral
B stadium
C wait
D memorie
E (No mistakes)

16
J refered
K ordinary
L blister
M exterior
N (No mistakes)

17
A scarcely
B surf
C born
D helth
E (No mistakes)

18
J exterior
K interval
L character
M privat
N (No mistakes)

STOP

Spelling

Lesson 3b **Spelling**

Directions: Fill in the space for any word that has a spelling mistake. If there is no mistake, fill in the last answer space.

Sample A	A	lecture
	B	industrial
	C	distribute
	D	grate
	E	(No mistakes)

Sample B	J	authorety
	K	customer
	L	style
	M	violet
	N	(No mistakes)

• **Look at the answer choices letter by letter. This is the best way to find spelling mistakes.**

1
A time
B promote
C theme
D individul
E (No mistakes)

2
J scarce
K conceal
L peice
M fountain
N (No mistakes)

3
A strickly
B cease
C vacant
D trait
E (No mistakes)

4
J suspect
K triangel
L bear
M velvet
N (No mistakes)

5
A pollution
B television
C recognize
D made
E (No mistakes)

6
J reknewed
K mechanical
L imagination
M package
N (No mistakes)

7
A theory
B procession
C budjet
D rode
E (No mistakes)

8
J according
K greedy
L dictionary
M waiste
N (No mistakes)

STOP

Answer rows
A Ⓐ B C D E   1 Ⓐ B C D E   3 Ⓐ B C D E   5 Ⓐ B C D E   7 Ⓐ B C D E
B Ⓙ K L M N   2 Ⓙ K L M N   4 Ⓙ K L M N   6 Ⓙ K L M N   8 Ⓙ K L M N

21

Test Yourself: Spelling

Unit 3

Directions: Fill in the space for any word that has a spelling mistake. If there is no mistake, fill in the last answer space.

Sample A			Sample B		
	A	serious		J	political
	B	anniversary		K	material
	C	horribel		L	berry
	D	league		M	cactus
	E	(No mistakes)		N	(No mistakes)

1
A bakery
B musician
C darken
D smileing
E (No mistakes)

2
J delicius
K radio
L golden
M cruel
N (No mistakes)

3
A monster
B southern
C depending
D thorn
E (No mistakes)

4
J absorb
K mishion
L haul
M cradle
N (No mistakes)

5
A mineral
B decorated
C superiure
D napkin
E (No mistakes)

6
J badge
K slippery
L purse
M guillty
N (No mistakes)

7
A further
B bearely
C toothbrush
D ranger
E (No mistakes)

8
J seledom
K wrinkle
L grasp
M dislike
N (No mistakes)

GO

9
A basement
B hairy
C electrisity
D spoken
E (No mistakes)

10
J midnight
K telescope
L cotton
M happiest
N (No mistakes)

11
A winter
B spoted
C friendship
D normally
E (No mistakes)

12
J picher
K trace
L skinny
M adventure
N (No mistakes)

13
A statement
B dough
C mystery
D timeing
E (No mistakes)

14
J battle
K harvest
L initeal
M remove
N (No mistakes)

15
A appearence
B punish
C continue
D measurement
E (No mistakes)

16
J avenue
K simple
L tasty
M lantren
N (No mistakes)

17
A result
B treaty
C charackter
D forest
E (No mistakes)

18
J suffering
K easily
L opposite
M honest
N (No mistakes)

STOP

Unit 4 Capitalization and Punctuation

Lesson 4a Capitalization

Directions: Fill in the space for the answer that has a mistake in capitalization. Fill in the last answer space if there is no mistake.

Sample A	A B C D	We spent a weekend in Vermont with Joanna's uncle. He owns a large dairy farm near Manchester. (No mistakes)
Sample B	J K L M	The state of iowa is known for its agriculture. The soil there is among the best in the world. (No mistakes)

• **Before you mark "No mistakes," check the answers one more time.**

1
A This year, Irma and her
B family are going to visit her
C grandmother on memorial day.
D (No mistakes)

2
J The swiss Alps are a mountain
K range in central Europe. They are
L known for skiing and colorful towns.
M (No mistakes)

3
A The last book I read was
B *african adventure.* Surprisingly,
C it isn't about Africa at all.
D (No mistakes)

4
J The teacher asked the children,
K "How many of you would like to
L go to the aquarium next week?"
M (No mistakes)

5
A During the debate, Antoine
B stated, "it is simply not true that
C most people spend too much money."
D (No mistakes)

6
J The Columbia River generates
K cheap electricity for much of the
L northwest part of the United States.
M (No mistakes)

7
A Rashid traveled from New York
B to Miami by Train. He made the
C return trip by plane with his aunt.
D (No mistakes)

8
J Golden Gate park, which is in
K San Francisco, is one of the
L most beautiful parks in the world.
M (No mistakes)

STOP

Unit 4

Capitalization and Punctuation

Lesson 4b Capitalization

Directions: Fill in the space for the answer that has a mistake in capitalization. Fill in the last answer space if there is no mistake.

Sample A	A	Our exchange student was from	Sample B	J	The apartment we rented is
	B	mexico. We enjoyed having her and		K	downtown. My mother usually
	C	hope to visit her home next year.		L	walks to work with aunt lara.
	D	(No mistakes)		M	(No mistakes)

• Before you mark "No mistakes," check the answers one more time.

1
A Luther visited france last
B year with a group of
C students from our school.
D (No mistakes)

2
J "this is not my idea of a good
K room," sighed Jawana as she looked
L at the tiny room with no windows.
M (No mistakes)

3
A The small island of Catalina
B is about 25 miles off the
C coast of southern California
D (No mistakes)

4
J 721 Shady brook Ln.
K Sebastopol, CA 95472
L July 17, 2001
M (No mistakes)

5
A dear Dad,
B The drive to Ashland was long, but
C the Meeks know some great car games.
D (No mistakes)

6
J Shane's dad stopped in the town
K of Dunsmuir. There was no attendant
L at the gas station, so we kept driving.
M (No mistakes)

7
A We found out later that the whole
B town was celebrating the opening of
C the annual Dunsmuir grower's market.
D (No mistakes)

8
J I guess that's life in a small town.
K your son,
L Damien
M (No mistakes)

STOP

Answer rows
A ⒶⒷⒸⒹ **1** ⒶⒷⒸⒹ **3** ⒶⒷⒸⒹ **5** ⒶⒷⒸⒹ **7** ⒶⒷⒸⒹ
B ⒿⓀⓁⓂ **2** ⒿⓀⓁⓂ **4** ⒿⓀⓁⓂ **6** ⒿⓀⓁⓂ **8** ⒿⓀⓁⓂ

25

Unit 4

Capitalization and Punctuation

Lesson 5a **Punctuation**

Directions: Fill in the space for the answer that has a mistake in punctuation. Fill in the last answer space if there is no mistake.

Sample A	A	Susan shouted to the others,
	B	Come over here! I think I
	C	found a good place to camp."
	D	(No mistakes)

Sample B	J	The storm that started on
	K	Sunday night is expected to
	L	last until at least Wednesday.
	M	(No mistakes)

- **Check for punctuation at the end of the sentence. Then look for a missing comma, apostrophe, or quotation mark in the sentence.**
- **Take your time and work carefully.**

1
A A large rock, which had been
B dug up during construction was
C washed and placed in the garden.
D (No mistakes)

2
J The school bus was parked
K near the museum. The children
L would meet there, at three o'clock.
M (No mistakes)

3
A Monday Tuesday and Wednesday
B are the best days to go to the movies.
C The other days are way too crowded.
D (No mistakes)

4
J The bridge over the river is
K being repaired. Traffic will be
L detoured to Second Street
M (No mistakes)

5
A "It is usually a good idea"
B to compare food prices among
C different stores before shopping.
D (No mistakes)

6
J How do you know what kind of
K bird that is? It looks just like
L every other bird at the bird feeder.
M (No mistakes)

7
A The bus driver said loudly, The
B next stop is Landis Avenue.
C Is anyone getting off there?"
D (No mistakes)

8
J Most of the furniture in
K the house has been borrowed
L from my mother aunt or sister.
M (No mistakes)

STOP

Unit 4

Capitalization and Punctuation

Lesson 5b **Punctuation**

Directions: Fill in the space for the answer that has a mistake in punctuation. Fill in the last answer space if there is no mistake.

Sample A	A	Stephen King is a famous
	B	writer who lives in Bangor Maine.
	C	I've read every one of his books.
	D	(No mistakes)

Sample B	J	As usual, Bill's bus was late.
	K	It was well past two oclock
	L	when it finally arrived.
	M	(No mistakes)

• **Remember, letters have special punctuation.**

1
A   We asked the magician how
B   the tricks were done? He cleverly
C   refused to give away his secrets.
D   (No mistakes)

2
J   The Iditarod an Alaskan dogsled
K   race, was won by a woman named
L   Libby Riddles in March of 1985.
M   (No mistakes)

3
A   Pinch these old blossoms right off,
B   Mrs. Calvi said to me in her garden.
C   "That allows the plant to bloom again."
D   (No mistakes)

4
J   14 Miles St
K   Denver, CO 80210
L   June 11, 2003
M   (No mistakes)

5
A   The Software Company
B   Arlington VA
C   Dear Mr. Howard,
D   (No mistakes)

6
J   Thank you for donating software
K   to our class. We enjoy using
L   your atlas and encyclopedia.
M   (No mistakes)

7
A   We have, however, experienced one
B   problem. The encyclopedia wont work
C   with our printer. Can you help us out?
D   (No mistakes)

8
J   I hope to hear from you soon.
K   Sincerely, yours
L   Rose Lindsay
M   (No mistakes)

STOP

Answer rows   **A** Ⓐ Ⓑ Ⓒ Ⓓ   **1** Ⓐ Ⓑ Ⓒ Ⓓ   **3** Ⓐ Ⓑ Ⓒ Ⓓ   **5** Ⓐ Ⓑ Ⓒ Ⓓ   **7** Ⓐ Ⓑ Ⓒ Ⓓ
　　　　　　　　　　B Ⓙ Ⓚ Ⓛ Ⓜ   **2** Ⓙ Ⓚ Ⓛ Ⓜ   **4** Ⓙ Ⓚ Ⓛ Ⓜ   **6** Ⓙ Ⓚ Ⓛ Ⓜ   **8** Ⓙ Ⓚ Ⓛ Ⓜ

Unit 4

Test Yourself: Capitalization and Punctuation

Directions: Fill in the space for the answer that has a mistake in capitalization or punctuation. Fill in the last answer space if there is no mistake.

Sample A
A The parade next week will
B begin at 9:00. We will meet you
C on Broad street near the bank.
D (No mistakes)

Sample B
J Don't worry about the dishes.
K We'll wash them when we get
L home from the football game.
M (No mistakes)

Directions: For questions 1–8, fill in the space for the answer that has a mistake in capitalization. Fill in the last answer space if there is no mistake.

1
A Half of the soccer team
B got a ride to the tournament
C in my father's volkswagen van.
D (No mistakes)

2
J The japanese launched a
K surprise attack on Pearl Harbor
L the morning of December 7, 1941.
M (No mistakes)

3
A City leaders in Portland, Oregon,
B are debating whether they should
C build a new Baseball Stadium there.
D (No mistakes)

4
J In the *golden compass* by Philip
K Pullman, a character named Lyra
L discovers who her real father is.
M (No mistakes)

5
A After we stuffed our sleeping bags and
B supplies into the car, Mom said,
C "it looks like there's no room left
   for us!"
D (No mistakes)

6
J One of the great American singers
K of the twentieth century was Mel Tormé,
L whose nickname was the velvet fog.
M (No mistakes)

7
A The poconos is the name of
B a mountain range and resort area
C located in the state of Pennsylvania.
D (No mistakes)

8
J My grandfather was very patriotic.
K He thought people should celebrate
L flag day every day, not just on June 14.
M (No mistakes)

GO

Directions: For questions 9–17, fill in the space for the answer that has a mistake in punctuation. Fill in the last answer space if there is no mistake.

9
A Have you ever said something
B you felt sorry about afterward.
C It pays to think before you speak.
D (No mistakes)

10
J The Fitches do their household
K chores on Saturday. If they finish by
L noon, they go to the hot dog stand.
M (No mistakes)

11
A We planted chives, peppermint,
B and sweet, basil in the herb garden
C along Grandmother's back fence.
D (No mistakes)

12
J Kathryn loved to hike.
K along the mountain path.
L She enjoyed peace and quiet.
M (No mistakes)

13
A Entertainer Sammy Davis Jr
B was famous for his skill as a singer,
C dancer, comedian, mimic, and actor.
D (No mistakes)

14
J 540 Chattham Ln
K Pittsfield, MA 01203
L May 20, 2001
M (No mistakes)

15
A Dear Zoe
B The neighborhood just had its annual
C yard sale. I sold a bunch of my old toys.
D (No mistakes)

16
J Business was slow the first hour, and
K I was about to give up Then things
L improved. My table was empty by two.
M (No mistakes)

17
A I sure wish you had been here.
B Your little sister
C Olivia
D (No mistakes)

STOP

Usage and Expression

Lesson 6a **Usage**

Directions: Fill in the space for the answer that has a mistake in usage. Fill in the last answer space if there is no mistake.

Sample A	A	The blew shirt goes well with
	B	your blazer. You want to look
	C	your best for your job interview.
	D	(No mistakes)

Sample B	J	Everyone in the neighborhood
	K	helped the family whose home
	L	had just been destroyed by fire.
	M	(No mistakes)

- **Read the answer choices to yourself carefully word by word. Use the meaning of the text to help you find the answer.**

- **If there are no mistakes, mark the last answer choice.**

1
A We wanted to put walnuts
B in the brownies, but there
C weren't none left in the pantry.
D (No mistakes)

2
J Me and Shana will do a science
K project about glass. We hope to
L make glass as part of the project.
M (No mistakes)

3
A Before she went camping, Ali
B went to the Outdoor Store and
C got her a new pair of hiking boots
D (No mistakes)

4
J This is the only kind of house paint
K they had at the store. It's not as
L better as the kind we bought before.
M (No mistakes)

5
A A submarine is a remarkable ship.
B It has everything people need
C to survive underwater for months.
D (No mistakes)

6
J Mina's father made a mistake when
K he built the deck, and now he
L has to take it apart and rebuild it.
M (No mistakes)

7
A If there is any left, I'd like
B another peace of pie. It is
C probably the best I've ever had.
D (No mistakes)

8
J Malvina wasn't sure to who she
K sent invitations because her list
L had been deleted from the computer.
M (No mistakes)

STOP

Usage and Expression

Directions: Fill in the space for the answer that has a mistake in usage. Fill in the last answer space if there is no mistake.

Sample **A**   A   If you call Regina and me at
        B   six o'clock, we will leave at once
        C   and meet you on Central Avenue.
        D   (No mistakes)

Sample **B**   J   Lots of people got stuck in
        K   traffic going to work this today
        L   but Mal and Brenda was on time.
        M   (No mistakes)

• If an item seems difficult, skip it and come back to it later.

1   A   We were all startled by the
    B   most loudest sound, but Holly
    C   said it was only a truck parking.
    D   (No mistakes)

2   J   Lee Ann's sister just won a
    K   scholarship to college. She is
    L   going to study civil engineering.
    M   (No mistakes)

3   A   We need something to
    B   put the dirt in, kinda like
    C   a large bucket or trash can.
    D   (No mistakes)

4   J   School ended on June seventh.
    K   By June ninth, workers were
    L   already fixing it up for next year.
    M   (No mistakes)

5   A   This bag of apples were on
    B   sale for two dollars. Last week,
    C   we had to pay over four dollars.
    D   (No mistakes)

6   J   Shevaun and Luis went down
    K   to the river. It took them an hour
    L   to find them a good place to fish.
    M   (No mistakes)

7   A   I was sure we were lost,
    B   but there was no one to ask
    C   witch way we should go.
    D   (No mistakes)

8   J   The delivery had came when
    K   no one was home, so the driver
    L   left the box with the neighbors.
    M   (No mistakes)

Answer rows   A   Ⓐ Ⓑ Ⓒ Ⓓ   **1**   Ⓐ Ⓑ Ⓒ Ⓓ   **3**   Ⓐ Ⓑ Ⓒ Ⓓ   **5**   Ⓐ Ⓑ Ⓒ Ⓓ   **7**   Ⓐ Ⓑ Ⓒ Ⓓ
               B   Ⓙ Ⓚ Ⓛ Ⓜ   **2**   Ⓙ Ⓚ Ⓛ Ⓜ   **4**   Ⓙ Ⓚ Ⓛ Ⓜ   **6**   Ⓙ Ⓚ Ⓛ Ⓜ   **8**   Ⓙ Ⓚ Ⓛ Ⓜ

31

Usage and Expression

Lesson 7a Expression

Sample A [1]The weeds are thick here. [2]We'll <u>have to pulling</u> them out before planting flowers.

What it the best way to write the underlined part of sentence 2?
A having to pull
B have to pull
C have pulled
D (No change)

- Remember, for this lesson, you are choosing the answer that is better than the others.

- Eliminate answer choices you know are wrong. If necessary, take your best guess from the remaining choices.

Directions: Use this paragraph to answer questions 1–4.

[1]The home office <u>has become</u> important for several reasons. [2]People are working longer hours, they must often contact others after normal business hours, and some even telecommute. [3]The <u>more important</u> room in the house is the kitchen. [4]A telecommuter is someone who works at home by using a telephone, fax machine, a computer, and overnight package delivery.

1 **Choose the best opening sentence to add to this paragraph.**
A Work is different today than before.
B Some people enjoy working in a home office, but others don't.
C Many working people now have an office at home.
D Different jobs require people to work in different places.

2 **What is the best way to write the underlined part of sentence 1?**
J become
K became
L was becoming
M (No change)

3 **Which sentence should be left out of this paragraph?**
A Sentence 1
B Sentence 2
C Sentence 3
D Sentence 4

4 **What is the best way to write the underlined part of sentence 3?**
J more importantly
K most important
L importanter
M (No change)

GO

Directions: For questions 5–8, choose the best way to express the idea.

5 A Parking his car in the lot, Mr. Gonzales to his office walked a block.
  B To his office Mr. Gonzales walked a block after parking his car.
  C In the lot Mr. Gonzales parked his car and to his office walked a block.
  D Mr. Gonzales parked his car in the lot and walked a block to his office.

6 J Most fruit trees have in the spring blossoms that turn into fruit later in the summer.
  K In the spring, most fruit trees have blossoms that turn into fruit later in the summer.
  L Later in the summer most fruit trees have fruit because in spring they had blossoms.
  M Turning into fruit later in summer, most fruit trees have blossoms in the spring.

7 A When we went to the beach, into the back of the car piled four of us.
  B Four of us piled into the back of the car when we went to the beach.
  C Into the back of the car when we went to the beach piled four of us.
  D When four of us piled into the back of the car, we to the beach went.

8 J The paint Vijay chose for his room was lighter than his parents wanted.
  K Vijay's parents wanted darker paint
      chosen by Vijay for his room.
  L For his room, Vijay chose paint which was lighter paint than his parents wanted.
  M Choosing lighter paint than his parents wanted, Vijay chose paint for his room.

9 **Which of these would be most appropriate in a thank-you letter?**

A The shirt you sent me is wonderful. It fits perfectly, and when I wear it to school, all of my friends like to talk about it because it was given to you by Arthur Ashe.

C The shirt you sent me fits fine. I wish it were a different color so it would go with my other clothes. I like to look nice when I go to school. Some of my friends don't care how they look.

B I like the shirt you sent me. Aunt Etta gave me a pair of pants that I wear when I play soccer. The pants are a great color. I play soccer almost every weekend.

D I got the shirt you sent me. One of the best parts about birthdays is getting presents. This year I got lots of them, but I wish I had gotten more money so I could buy things myself.

Directions: Fill in the space for the answer that is better than the others.

Sample A   My mother's hobby, **making** pottery, has become a business for her.
   A   to making   B   to make   C   having made   D   (No change)

Sample B   Adrian called you this morning, **but** she didn't leave a message.
   J   or   K   because   L   so   M   (No change)

• **Pay attention to the directions for each section.**

1   **Unless** good software, a computer is almost useless.
   A   Except   B   Although   C   Without   D   (No change)

2   By the end of next year, Ellen **will have saved** more than $5,000 in her college fund.
   J   saving   K   saved   L   to save   M   (No change)

3   My dog, Ollie, follows me **whichever** I go.
   A   however   B   wherever   C   ever where   D   (No change)

4   **Which of these would be most appropriate at the end of a report about the pyramids in Egypt?**

J	In the desert sands of Egypt are some of the most remarkable structures in the world. Called pyramids, they are tombs for the ancient rulers of Egypt.	L	Some of the pyramids were built as long as five thousand years ago. Scientists still do not know how the Egyptians moved such huge pieces of stone.
K	The weather has not been kind to the pyramids. Even though they were built well, the wind, sun, and rain have caused a great deal of damage.	M	Even though scientists have studied the pyramids for hundreds of years, some mysteries remain. Perhaps they will be solved by future research.

GO

Directions: Use this paragraph to answer questions 5–10.

¹The red-breasted robin is perhaps the most well-known American bird. ²Another well-known bird is the starling. ³In the summer, its range <u>extends</u> well into northern Canada. ⁴In the winter, the robin heads to the southern part of the United States. ⁵It feeds mostly on insects, and <u>often being seen</u> in grassy areas looking for its favorite food, the garden worm.

5 **Which sentence should be left out of this paragraph?**
A Sentence 1
B Sentence 2
C Sentence 3
D Sentence 4

6 **What is the best way to write the underlined part of sentence 3?**
J extending
K to extend
L had extended
M (No change)

7 **What is the best way to write the underlined part of sentence 5?**
A can often be seen
B to be often seen
C can often to be seen
D (No change)

8 **Choose the best concluding sentence to add to this paragraph.**
J It is truly amazing how far some birds can fly.
K Both the robin and the starling live in large cities.
L The robin lays 3 or 4 blue eggs in a well-made nest lined with feathers.
M Many other birds feed mostly on different kinds of seeds.

9 **Which of these is the best sentence to add to the paragraph?**
A Other birds will come to a feeder if you put food in it.
B For many people, the robin is a sure sign of spring.
C A blue jay is a little larger than a robin and is a different color.
D Northern Canada is too cold in winter for most birds.

10 **Where is the best place for sentence 5?**
J Where it is now.
K Between sentences 1 and 2
L Between sentences 2 and 3
M Before sentence 1.

STOP

Unit 5

Test Yourself: Usage and Expression

Directions: Fill in the space for the answer that has a mistake in usage. Fill in the last answer space if there is no mistake.

Sample A
- A It doesn't do much good to
- B have a swimming pool in the
- C yard if you can't never use it.
- D (No mistakes)

Sample B
- J The two workers mixed the bags
- K of concrete in a tub. Then they
- L poured it into wooden frames.
- M (No mistakes)

1
- A My friend, Alec, bought
- B hisself a new CD player with
- C money he earned last summer.
- D (No mistakes)

2
- J Best friends have disagreements
- K from time to time, but that's never
- L been a problem for Pamela and I.
- M (No mistakes)

3
- A After taking a speech class,
- B most of the students speaked
- C with greater confidence and skill.
- D (No mistakes)

4
- J Favian Escobar proved that
- K it was possible for a sixth grader
- L to become a famous chess master.
- M (No mistakes)

5
- A Let's do something active this
- B weekend. How's about going
- C for a canoe ride on the river?
- D (No mistakes)

6
- J Because he had so much
- K to do before the big game,
- L Barney had rose early that day.
- M (No mistakes)

7
- A A tire swing hangs from the oak
- B tree behind my house. It has hanged
- C there ever since I was a little kid.
- D (No mistakes)

8
- J Some of my friends get rewards
- K for bringing home good grades, but I
- L don't get nothing except self-respect.
- M (No mistakes)

9
- A I had almost succeeded at
- B keeping my birthday a secret, but
- C you done gone and told everyone.
- D (No mistakes)

10
- J It didn't look like nobody was
- K home. No lights were turned
- L on and no cars were in the driveway.
- M (No mistakes)

GO

---

36   **Answer rows**   A Ⓐ Ⓑ Ⓒ Ⓓ   1 Ⓐ Ⓑ Ⓒ Ⓓ   3 Ⓐ Ⓑ Ⓒ Ⓓ   5 Ⓐ Ⓑ Ⓒ Ⓓ   7 Ⓐ Ⓑ Ⓒ Ⓓ   9 Ⓐ Ⓑ Ⓒ Ⓓ
       B Ⓙ Ⓚ Ⓛ Ⓜ   2 Ⓙ Ⓚ Ⓛ Ⓜ   4 Ⓙ Ⓚ Ⓛ Ⓜ   6 Ⓙ Ⓚ Ⓛ Ⓜ   8 Ⓙ Ⓚ Ⓛ Ⓜ   10 Ⓙ Ⓚ Ⓛ Ⓜ

Directions: Use this paragraph to answer questions 11–16.

¹ To start a business, you need some money and a lot of dedication. ²At first, you <u>had to work</u> long hours. ³After a time, you may reach the point where you can <u>hire</u> employees. ⁴When the business succeeds, you will be able to earn a decent living. ⁵Making a lot of money will let you buy the things you want. ⁶You will also feel good <u>although you are able to</u> give other people jobs.

11 **Choose the best opening sentence to add to this paragraph.**
- A   Small businesses can sometimes be very successful.
- B   Starting your own business is hard work, but it is rewarding.
- C   Work is how you earn money.
- D   Many people have jobs they enjoy.

12 **What is the best way to write the underlined part of sentence 2?**
- J   having to work
- K   to be working
- L   will have to work
- M   (No change)

13 **Which sentence should be left out of this paragraph?**
- A   Sentence 3
- B   Sentence 4
- C   Sentence 5
- D   Sentence 6

14 **What is the best way to write the underlined part of sentence 3?**
- J   hired
- K   hires
- L   have hired
- M   (No change)

15 **What is the best way to write the underlined part of sentence 6?**
- A   except being able
- B   because you are able
- C   if you can be able
- D   (No change)

16 **Choose the best concluding sentence to add to this paragraph.**
- J   For many people, starting a business is the greatest challenge of their life.
- K   Be sure to choose a business you like, because you might actually succeed.
- L   When you hire employees, you will have to pay them fairly and have good working conditions.
- M   Small business sometimes grow into larger ones.

GO

Directions: For questions 17–21, choose the best way of writing the idea.

17 A A popular song, "Happy Birthday," written by Mildred and Patty Hill.
   B The popular Mildred and Patty Hill wrote it, the "Happy Birthday" song.
   C The popular "Happy Birthday" song was written by Mildred and Patty Hill.
   D It was written and popular, "Happy Birthday" by Mildred and Patty Hill.

18 J Newborn baby robins, they have a diet of about 14 daily worms.
   K Newborn baby robins eat on average just about 14 worms each day.
   L Baby robins eat approximately 14 worms in one single day.
   M Baby robins eat approximately 14 worms a day.

19 A The book for which you are looking on the table in the living room.
   B The book you are looking for is on the table in the living room.
   C In the living room, on the table, the book for which you are looking.
   D Looking for the book on the table in the living room.

20 J We now have hundreds of tadpoles in our pond, although a frog laid eggs.
   K A frog laid eggs in our pond because now we have hundreds of tadpoles.
   L A frog laid eggs in our pond, and now we have hundreds of tadpoles.
   M In our pond, a frog laid eggs, except now we have hundreds of tadpoles.

21 A Bonnie spends Saturday morning volunteering at the animal shelter.
   B At the animal shelter, Bonnie spends Saturday morning volunteering.
   C Volunteering on Saturday morning, Bonnie spends it at the animal shelter.
   D On Saturday morning at the animal shelter, Bonnie spends it volunteering.

22 **Which of these would be most appropriate in a letter from a student who wants to interview a newly elected official for a school paper?**

J I write for our school paper. The paper is published once a month. It goes to all of the students, and they usually bring it home to their parents. I do interviews with different people.	L Because you have just been elected, I would like to interview you for our school paper. I would be happy to come to your office for the interview at a time that is good for you.
K I would like to interview you. Our school has a paper. It is published by the students. I write for the paper. The interview wouldn't take long. I usually interview other students.	M You have just been elected. I would like to do an interview with you. I am busy with school, so you will have to come to school when I am available. I hope this isn't too much trouble.

GO

Directions: For questions 23–27, choose the best way to write the underlined part of the sentence.

23 The tournament officials disliked **to turning away** anyone.

A having to turn away   B to turn away   C turned away   D (No change)

24 Don't go out after school **except** telling me where you will be.

J although   K without   L unless   M (No change)

25 **Being late** is a terrible way to start a job interview.

A Going to be late   B Being lately   C Will be late   D (No change)

26 **Because** I had met him before, I had trouble recognizing him.

J Since   K Unless   L Although   M (No change)

27 Careful planning will make a camping trip **safely** and enjoyable.

A safer   B safe   C safety   D (No change)

28 Which of these would be most appropriate as the opening for a history project?

J | London is a large city in England. Do you think you would like to visit there? It is like many large cities in the United States.

L | The people in London come from all over the world. That is because England used to have colonies around the world.

K | Most people don't know the history of London. They probably don't know much about the history of their own town or city.

M | The city of London had its beginning more than 2,000 years ago. It was a small town then, nothing like the city of today.

STOP

Math Concepts and Estimation

Lesson 8a Math Concepts

Sample A Which is a reasonable estimate of the height of a regular door?

    A   2 meters

    B   3 feet

    C   4 yards

    D   5 centimeters

Sample B What number is between 654 and 667?

    J   653

    K   676

    L   656

    M   672

TIPS

- Look carefully at the numbers and figures for each problem.
- Read the question, look at the answer choices, then read the problem again. This will help you find the answer.

1 The numbers in the tables below are related by the same rule. What number is missing in the second table?

Table 1	0	1	2	2	4	8	9
Table 2	0	4	8	8	16	32	?

    A   33   C   36

    B   35   D   38

2 A fly is circling over the target below. On which part is it most likely to land?

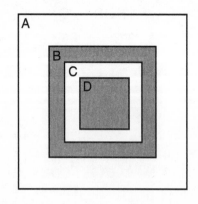

    J   A   L   B

    K   C   M   D

3 Which figure below is a parallelogram?

4 In which figure is angle *ABC* exactly 90°?

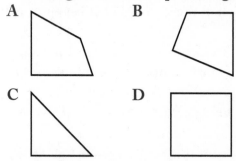

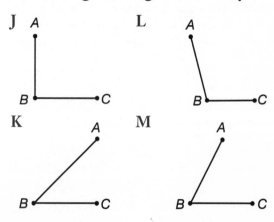

GO →

5 Which is the value of *a* if $\frac{12}{a} = 3$?

   A 2   C 4

   B 3   D 6

6 Which numeral has the same value as $\frac{21}{5}$?

   J 4   L $4\frac{1}{2}$

   K $4\frac{1}{5}$ M $5\frac{1}{5}$

7 What should replace the _ to make the number sentence true?

$$(9 + \_) + 1 = (1 + 4) + 9$$

   A 1

   B 2

   C 3

   D 4

8 What should replace the △ in the multiplication problem on the right?

   J 5

   K 6

   L 8

   M 9

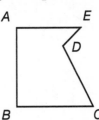

```
    1 4 5
  ×   4 1
    1 4 5
  5 △ 0
  5 □ 4 5
```

9 Which is the greatest common factor of 21 and 35?

   A 3   C 7

   B 6   D 9

10 Which is another way of writing fourteen hundredths?

   J 0.014

   K 0.14

   L 1.4

   M 14

11 Which set of numbers has the greatest average (mean)?

   A {1, 2, 9}   C {2, 5, 9}

   B {2, 4, 8}   D {5, 7, 9}

12 The figures below are congruent. Which pair of parts is identical?

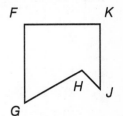

   J *DE* and *HJ*   L *BC* and *GH*

   K *AE* and *GH*   M *CD* and *KJ*

GO ▶

13 Which figure is missing in this pattern?

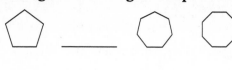

A ◯

C ⬡ (octagon)

B ▢

D ⬡ (hexagon)

14 The best unit for measuring the number of people in New York City is

J   tens of people.
K   hundreds of people.
L   thousands of people.
M   millions of people.

15 What should replace the △ to make the number sentence true?

$(2 + 9) \times \triangle < 43$

A   3
B   4
C   5
D   6

16 Which of the following statements is true?

J $\frac{1}{8} > \frac{1}{7}$

K $\frac{1}{3} < \frac{1}{5}$

L $\frac{1}{8} < \frac{1}{4}$

M $\frac{1}{5} > \frac{1}{4}$

17 About what fraction of the figure is shaded?

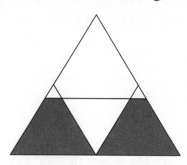

A   Less than $\frac{1}{4}$

B   Between $\frac{1}{4}$ and $\frac{1}{2}$

C   Between $\frac{1}{2}$ and $\frac{3}{4}$

D   More than $\frac{3}{4}$

18 How should the numeral 489.231 be written if it is rounded to the nearest hundredth?

J   490
K   489
L   489.2
M   489.23

STOP

Math Concepts and Estimation

Lesson 8b Math Concepts

Directions: Read each mathematics problem. Choose the answer that is better than the others.

Sample A Which fraction is not equal to 0.25?

A $\frac{1}{2}$

B $\frac{1}{4}$

C $\frac{2}{8}$

D $\frac{3}{12}$

Sample B If c is a positive number, what should replace the $\square$ to make the equation true?

$$c \times 1 = \square$$

J   0

K   1

L   c

M   d

- **Sometimes you can solve a problem by thinking. You don't have to compute to find the answer.**

1 Roy was playing with a six-sided game block. The first time he rolled a 3. What is the chance that he also rolled a 3 the second time?

A $\frac{1}{5}$

B $\frac{5}{6}$

C $\frac{1}{6}$

D $\frac{1}{12}$

2 Which is the correct solution to

$$0.7 \times \square = 0.42$$

J   0.06

K   0.6

L   6

M   60

3 The numbers in the table below are related to each other by the same rule. What number is missing in the second row?

Row 1	1	5	9	14	18
Row 2	24	28	$\square$	37	41

A   14

B   32

C   34

D   45

4 When $a = 5$ and $b = 7$, which of these is the value of $3a + 6b$?

J   21

K   40

L   57

M   63

GO

5 Which solid figure could be formed using all the pieces at the right?

A   A cylinder
B   A cube
C   A pyramid
D   A cone

6 The set of numbers {2, 4, 9, 16, 25, 36, 49, 64, 81} can be described as a set of
J   prime numbers.
K   even numbers.
L   squares of numbers.
M   factors of 160.

7 If $60 \div s = 15$, what is the value of $15 \times s$?
A s
B   4
C   15
D   60

8 If the product of two whole numbers is 25, which of the following best describes the numbers?
J   Both are odd.
K   Both are even.
L   One is even and one is odd.
M   There is not enough information to tell.

9 Camille has 4 yellow buttons, 3 brown buttons, 3 green buttons, and 2 blue buttons in a jar. If she takes buttons out of the jar without looking, at most how many buttons will she have to take before she gets 2 buttons of the same color?
A   4
B   5
C   6
D   12

10 If c is a positive number, what should replace the □ to make the equation true?
$\frac{c}{1} = $ □
J c
K d
L   0
M   1

11 Which number is between 3,861 and 4,259?
A   3,816
B   3,859
C   4,195
D   4,295

12 Karen ran the first mile of a race in 9 minutes and the second mile in 11 minutes. What was her average speed for the two miles?
J   2 minutes
K   5 minutes
L   10 minutes
M   20 minutes

13 If the 4 in 4,971 is changed to an 8, how is the value of the number changed?
A   It increases by 4.
B   It increases by 4,000.
C   It increases by 8.
D   It increases by 8,000.

14 If you add two odd numbers together, what is true about their sum?
J   It must be odd.
K   It must be even.
L   It may be even or odd.
M   It will be a prime number.

STOP

Math Concepts and Estimation

Lesson 9a Estimation

Directions: Choose the answer that is the best estimate of the exact answer.

Sample A   The closest estimate of
5.12 + 2.88 + 3.02 is _____ .
A   1.1
B   11
C   111
D   1,111

Sample B   The closest estimate of 782 × 130
is _____ .
J   700 × 100
K   700 × 200
L   800 × 200
M   800 × 100

- Be sure you understand what you are supposed to do.
- The correct answer will be an estimate, not an exact answer.

1   The closest estimate of 24,187 + 16,032
is between _____ .
A   39,000 and 40,000
B   40,000 and 41,000
C   41,000 and 42,000
D   42,000 and 43,000

2   Scissors cost $7.95. The closest estimate of
the change you would receive if you paid for
the scissors with a $20 bill is _____ .
J $9
K $10
L $11
M $12

3   One baseball costs $6.29. One golf
ball costs $1.69. Total cost of three balls
is $14.75. The closest estimate of the
cost of the third ball is _____ .
A $5
B $6
C $7
D $8

4   A frog's average jump is 18 inches. The
closest estimate of how far a frog will go
in 5 jumps is _____ .
J   60 inches
K   100 inches
L   110 inches
M   120 inches

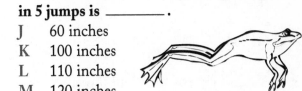

5   The closest estimate of 321 + 275 + 479
is _____ .
A   300 + 300 + 500
B   300 + 200 + 500
C   300 + 400 + 400
D   200 + 200 + 400

6   The closest estimate of 1,930 ÷ 5
is _____ .
J   200 and 250
K   250 and 300
L   300 and 350
M   350 and 400

STOP

Answer rows   A ⒶⒷⒸⒹ   1 ⒶⒷⒸⒹ   3 ⒶⒷⒸⒹ   5 ⒶⒷⒸⒹ
                 B ⒿⓀⓁⓂ   2 ⒿⓀⓁⓂ   4 ⒿⓀⓁⓂ   6 ⒿⓀⓁⓂ

Directions: Choose the answer that is the best estimate of the exact answer.

Sample A The closest estimate of
2.9 + 4.1 is _____.
A   10
B   11
C   12
D   13

Sample B There are 12 inches in a foot. The
closest estimate of how many inches
are in 9 feet is _____.
J   80
K   90
L   100
M   190

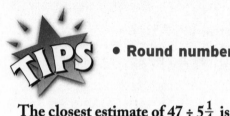

• Round numbers before you compute to find the answer.

1 The closest estimate of $47 \div 5\frac{1}{4}$ is _____.
A   18
B   19
C   10
D   11

2 A candle burns for 50 minutes.
The closest estimate of how long
5 candles will burn is _____.
J   Less than 3 hours
K   Between 3 and 4 hours
L   Between 4 and 5 hours
M   More than 5 hours

3 The closest estimate of 71,926 ÷ 9
is _____.
A   8,000
B   80,000
C   800,000
D   800,0000

4 The speedometer above
shows the current speed
of a car. The driver
increases her speed by
15 miles per hour. The
closest estimate of the
new speed of the car is _____.
J   about 50 miles per hour
K   between 50 and 55 miles per hour
L   about 60 miles per hour
M   more than 65 miles per hour

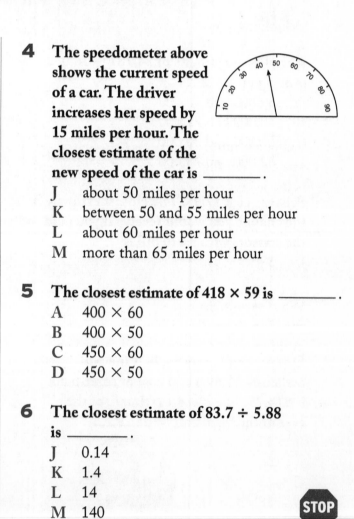

5 The closest estimate of 418 × 59 is _____.
A   400 × 60
B   400 × 50
C   450 × 60
D   450 × 50

6 The closest estimate of 83.7 ÷ 5.88
is _____.
J   0.14
K   1.4
L   14
M   140

STOP

Test Yourself: Math Concepts and Estimation

Sample A On a scale, 1 unit represents 10 pounds. If a sack of flour weighs 50 pounds, what is the reading on the scale?

  A 1 unit
  B 5 units
  C 10 units
  D 500 units

Sample B A shelf is 3-feet 10-inches wide. There are 8 books per foot. The closest estimate of the number of books on the shelf is _____ .

  J 20
  K 30
  L 40
  M 50

Directions: For questions 1–21, read each mathematics problem. Choose the answer that is better than the others.

1 Which number is between 3,478 and 3,721?

  A 3,425
  B 3,445
  C 3,511
  D 3,724

2 Kalila has one dog that weighs 70 pounds and one dog that weighs 30 pounds. What is the average weight of the 2 dogs?

  J 30 pounds
  K 50 pounds
  L 70 pounds
  M 110 pounds

3 What should replace the △ in the multiplication problem shown at right?

  A 0
  B 1
  C 8
  D 9

$$
\begin{array}{r}
272 \\
\times\ 44 \\
\hline
1088 \\
10\triangle8 \\
\hline
11968 \\
\end{array}
$$

4 If the 9 in 2,971 is changed to a 4, how is the value of the number changed?

  J The number increases by 400.
  K The number increases by 500.
  L The number decreases by 400.
  M The number decreases by 500.

5 How many blocks are needed to make the figure below?

  A 6
  B 10
  C 15
  D 30

6 Raquelle is going to see a concert at 7:15 P.M. and it is 3:45 P.M. now. How long does Raquelle have to wait before the concert starts?

  J 4 hours and 30 minutes
  K 4 hours and 60 minutes
  L 3 hours and 30 minutes
  M 3 hours and 15 minutes

GO

7 Reading from left to right, which numerals are represented by the △, □, and ☆ on the number line below?

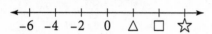

A   1, 3, 5

B   5, 3, 1

C $\frac{1}{5}, \frac{1}{4}, \frac{1}{3}$

D $\frac{1}{3}, \frac{1}{4}, \frac{1}{5}$

8 Which is the same as four hundred twenty-three thousand, five hundred seventy-eight?

J   423,578

K   40,023,578

L   40,023,000,578

M   400,230,050,078

9 The best unit for measuring the cost of a new house is

A   tens of dollars.

B   hundreds of dollars.

C   thousands of dollars.

D   millions of dollars.

10 What should replace the □ to make the number sentence true?

$$(2+5) \times \square < 38$$

J   5   L   7

K   6   M   8

11 Which of the following statements is true?

A $\frac{1}{4} > \frac{1}{3}$

B $\frac{1}{5} < \frac{1}{6}$

C $\frac{1}{9} < \frac{1}{5}$

D $\frac{1}{7} > \frac{1}{6}$

12 How should the numeral 123.831 be written if it is rounded to the nearest hundredth?

J   100

K   120

L   123.8

M   123.83

13 The set of numbers {1, 2, 4, 8, 16, 32, 64} can best be described as a set of

A   prime numbers.

B   even numbers.

C   squares of numbers.

D   factors of 64.

14 Which fraction is not equal to 0.2?

J $\frac{1}{3}$

K $\frac{1}{5}$

L $\frac{2}{10}$

M $\frac{4}{20}$

15 Which figure is missing in this pattern?

A   C

B   D

GO

16 Which is the correct solution to
$$0.6 \times \square = 0.48$$
J   0.08
K   0.8
L   8
M   80

17 The numbers in the table below are related to each other by the same rule. What number is missing from the second row?

Row 1	1	2	4	8	16
Row 2	2	$\square$	8	16	32

A   1
B   3
C   4
D   16

18 When $a = 4$ and $b = 5$, which of these is the value of $3a + 4b$?
J   16
K   28
L   32
M   35

19 If $24 \div s = 4$, what is the value of $4 \times s$?
A s
B   4
C   6
D   24

20 A measurement of 3.1 kilometers probably describes the length of a
J   pencil.
K   city bus.
L   cross-country race.
M   swimming pool.

21 About what fraction of the figure is shaded?
A   Less than $\frac{1}{8}$
B   Between $\frac{1}{8}$ and $\frac{1}{4}$
C   Between $\frac{1}{4}$ and $\frac{1}{2}$
D   More than $\frac{1}{2}$

GO

Directions: For questions 22–32, choose the answer that is the best estimate of the exact answer.

22 $437 \div 61$ is _____ .

   J   less than 4
   K   between 4 and 6
   L   between 6 and 8
   M   more than 8

23 It costs $22.84 to groom Patty's dog. It costs $17.13 to groom Ralph's dog. About how much more will it cost to groom Patty's dog than Ralph's dog?

   A $6
   B $7
   C $8
   D $9

24 The closest estimate of $2\frac{5}{9} + 6\frac{4}{7}$ is _____ .

   J   8
   K   9
   L   10
   M   11

25 The average number of students per school = 876. The number of schools in the district = 28. The closest estimate of how many students are in the district is _____ .

   A   2,700
   B   20,700
   C   27,000
   D   270,000

26 $24.15 × 19 is _____ .

   J   less than $200
   K   more than $700
   L   between $300 and $500
   M   between $500 and $700

GO

27 The price of 1 pound of strawberries is $1.29. A man buys $11.78 worth of strawberries. The number of pounds of strawberries purchased is _____.

A less than 8
B between 8 and 9
C between 9 and 10
D more than 10

28 The closest estimate of 42,085 + 19,892 is _____.

J 6,000
K 60,000
L 600,000
M 6,000,000

29 The closest estimate of $46.23 ÷ 5 is _____.

A $7
B $8
C $9
D $10

30 The closest estimate of 473 × 45 is _____.

J 500 × 40
K 400 × 40
L 400 × 50
M 500 × 50

31 The closest estimate of 375 ÷ 62 is _____.

A 5
B 6
C 7
D 8

32 The closest estimate of 614 ÷ 23 is _____.

J 30
K 300
L 3,000
M 30,000

STOP

Math Problem Solving and Data Interpretation

Lesson 10a Math Problem Solving

Directions: Read each mathematics problem. Choose the answer that is better than the others.

Item	Regular Price	Sale Price
Shirts	$ 22	$ 15
Pants	$ 25	$ 22
Shoes	$ 30	$ 21
Socks	$ 3	$ 2
Belts	$ 8	$ 5

Sample A How much would it cost to buy one pair of pants and two shirts at the sale price?
A $48
B $59
C $69
D Not given

- Read the question and think about what you are supposed to do.
- Solve the problem on scratch paper. If your answer is not one of the choices, work it again.

Directions: Cliff's Amusement Park advertised special prices for the end of school. Use the advertisement below to answer questions 1–4.

Cliff's Amusement Park End-of-School Special
One Ticket $0.25
Book of Ten Tickets $2.00
Book of Fifty Tickets $9.00
Family Pack (100 Tickets) $20.00

STUDENT SPECIAL
Bring a friend and get a **FREE** book of ten tickets with each book of fifty tickets purchased at the regular price.

1 How much would you save if you bought a Family Pack instead of 10 packs of ten tickets?
A Nothing
B $5.00
C $10.00
D Not given

2 Karen and Joe want to take advantage of the student special. They will split the cost of the special and share the tickets equally. How much will they each have to pay?
J $2.00
K $4.00
L $6.00
M Not given

3 Each ride at Cliff's costs 2 tickets. How could you find out how many rides each member of a family can take if they bought the Family Pack?
A Divide 100 by the number of family members then multiply by two.
B Divide 100 by the number of family members then divide by 2.
C Multiply 100 by 2 then multiply by the number of family members.
D It cannot be determined.

GO

4 Which way to buy tickets gives you the lowest price per ticket?

J   One Ticket
K   Book of Ten Tickets
L   Book of Fifty Tickets
M   Family Pack (100 Tickets)

5 Neysa is planning to buy a camera. At the Camera Club, it is on sale for $129.95. The Camera Hut advertises low prices every day. What information does Neysa need to decide which camera to buy?

A   The regular price at Camera Club
B   The percent discount at Camera Club
C   The price of the camera at Camera Hut
D   The percent discount at Camera Hut

6 Neysa bought 6 rolls of film for her camera. Each roll takes 24 pictures. How many pictures can Neysa take with the film she bought?

J   124
K   150
L   154
M   Not given

7 To develop one roll of film costs $6.50. If you want double prints, it costs just one dollar more. How much will Neysa pay to develop three rolls of film and get double prints for all of them?

A $22.50
B $23.50
C $25.50
D   Not given

8 When Neysa took her first roll of 36 pictures, she had some problems. She overexposed 3 pictures and forgot to take the lens cap off for 2 pictures. How can she find the number of pictures she took right?

J   Multiply 3 times 2 then subtract the product from 36.
K   Add 3 and 2 then subtract the sum from 36.
L   Add 3 and 2 then subtract 36.
M   Add 3 and 2 and 36.

9 Some children gathered a total of 500 pounds of newspapers for recycling. They are tying the papers up in bundles of 30 pounds each. How many bundles of papers will they end up with?

A   16
B   17
C   18
D   Not given

10 The recycling center pays $.25 a pound for aluminum cans. Julia and Mario collected 327 pounds of cans, but 142 were made of steel. How much will they be paid for the cans they collected?

J $35.50
K $45.25
L $81.75
M   Not given

11 At the end of the year, Julia and Mario had earned a total of $490. They split this money equally. Which of these would Julia be able to buy with her share and have the least left over?

A   A mountain bike for $240
B   A racing bike for $320
C   A television for $445
D   A computer for $785

STOP

Unit 7

Math Problem Solving and Data Interpretation

Lesson 10b Math Problem Solving

Directions: Read each mathematics problem. Choose the answer that is better than the others.

Sample A	Mrs. Link teaches 4 Spanish classes with 25 students in each class. Her students do interclass projects that involve 20 students per group. How many project groups can be formed by the students in all of her classes?	A	6
		B	7
		C	10
		D	Not given

- Take your time when you try to answer a question.
- Be sure you understand what the question is asking.

1 Mrs. Link teaches 4 Spanish classes with 25 students in each class. Her students do interclass projects that involve 20 students per group. Mrs. Link had the students practice dialogues. All of the students in one class took part in the dialogue, which was 10 minutes long. In the class, there were 5 groups of 3 and the rest were in groups of 2. How can Mrs. Link find out the number of students who worked in groups of 2?

A Subtract 15 from 25
B Subtract 8 from 10
C Subtract 15 from 25 and then divide the answer by 2
D Subtract 10 from 25 and then divide by 3

2 Mrs. Link is planning a field trip to a Mexican restaurant. Some of the students will be going on Thursday and some will be going on Friday. There are more students going on Thursday than Friday. Which of the following pieces of information is needed to allow Mrs. Link to figure out how many students in the morning class are going on Thursday?

J The total number of students going on Thursday in all 4 of Mrs. Link's classes
K The total number of students in the morning class
L The total number of students in all 4 of Mrs. Link's classes
M The total number of students in the morning class going on Friday

GO ➡

3   The students in one class are planning a fiesta for the end of school. Nine students will bring in dried fruit for the piñata. The other students will be in pairs, and each pair will bring a game to play. How many pairs of students are bringing in games?

A   8
B   8
C   16
D   Not given

4   Oliver practices 3 songs in 1 hour. Kelly practices twice as many songs in the same time. How many songs can Kelly practice in 3 hours?

J   6
K   9
L   12
M   18

5   Kelly and Oliver were practicing for a music recital. Kelly played 5 songs a day for 5 days and Oliver played 6 songs a day for 3 days. How many songs did they play in all?

A   11
B   43
C   45
D   Not given

6   Oliver's music teacher charges $10.00 for a 30 minute lesson. Kelly's music teacher charges $8.50 for a 30 minute lesson. How much could Oliver save on a 90 minute lesson by going to Kelly's music teacher?

J $1.50
K $3.00
L $4.50
M   Not given

STOP

Math Problem Solving and Data Interpretation

Lesson 11a Data Interpretation

Directions: Read each mathematics problem. Choose the answer that is better than the others.

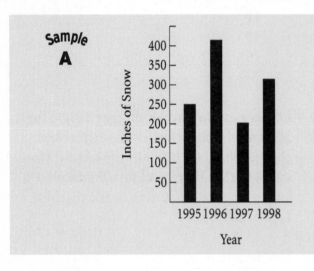

Sample A

The graph shows the amount of snow that fell in a mountain town during four years. In which year did more than 400 inches of snow fall?

A   1995
B   1996
C   1997
D   1998

TIPS

- **Read each question carefully. Be sure you understand what you are supposed to do.**
- **Look at the graph or chart to find the answer.**

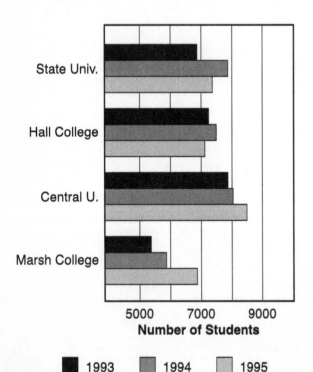

1993   1994   1995

1 About how many students attended State Univ. in 1994?
A   6900
B   7400
C   7900
D   8200

2 In 1995, how many more students attended Central U. than Hall College?
J   1300
K   1500
L   2300
M   2500

3 Which college has the smallest number of students?
A   State Univ.
B   Hall College
C   Central U.
D   Marsh College

GO

Directions: This graph shows how many people were in a department store each hour during a day. Use the graph to answer questions 4–7.

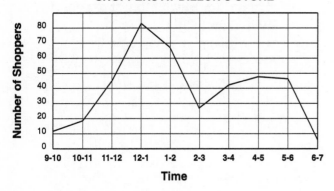

SHOPPERS AT DILLON'S STORE

4 Which of these is true about the morning hours in the store?

J   The number of people increases each hour.

K   The number of people decreases each hour.

L   The number of people stays about the same each hour.

M   The early morning is busier than the later morning.

5 About how many shoppers come into the store during the 12 to 1 time period?

A   72

B   78

C   82

D   88

6 How many fewer customers were in the store during the 2–3 time period than in the 1–2 time period?

J   25

K   20

L   35

M   40

7 The store manager wants to close the store for an hour each day. Based on the number of customers, which time period should she choose?

A   10–11

B   12–1

C   2–3

D   6–7

GO

Lesson 11b Data Interpretation

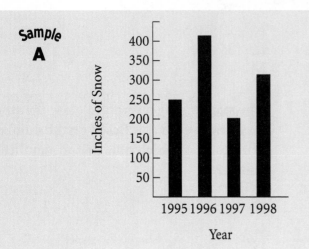

Sample A

Inches of Snow / Year

About how much more snow fell in 1996 than in 1997?
A   two times as much
B   three times as much
C   four times as much
D   five times as much

- **Read each question carefully. Be sure you understand what you are supposed to do.**

- **Look at the graph or chart to find the answer.**

Directions: This table shows the population, average family size, and average family income of some towns. Use the table to answer questions 1–3.

City	Population	Family Size	Family Income
Bernardo	15,327	4.6	$19,374
Pauley	7,915	3.1	$18,657
Stargo	8,463	3.6	$18,316
Plainville	9,082	4.5	$20,178
Maple Grove	17,618	4.8	$19,286
Statler	6571	4.2	$20,221
Parsenne	14,294	4.4	$21,904
Regis	7,136	3.9	$18,831
Dixon	8,729	3.9	$20,432
Ashland	12,720	3.3	$18,559

1   What is the difference in family income between Maple Grove and Dixon?
A $211
B $925
C $1,146
D $1,156

2   Which city has a family size that is less than that of Stargo?
J   Bernardo
K   Ashland
L   Dixon
M   Plainville

3   Which of these cities has a family income between $18,500 and $19,000?
A   Ashland
B   Stargo
C   Bernardo
D   Maple Grove

STOP

Directions: Use the list below to answer the questions.

Sample A How much more does a plant from shelf 1 cost than a plant from shelf 4?
A $7.75
B $10.00
C $12.25
D   Not given

Sample B Rashmi bought 4 plants from shelf 4 at the sale. How much did she spend?
J $3.00
K $8.25
L $9.00
M   Not given

Directions: Andrea's parent's opened up a garden supply store and they are having a grand opening sale. The items below are for sale. Use this list to answer questions 1–5.

Potted Plants	
Shelf 1	$10.00
Shelf 2	$7.25
Shelf 3	$5.00
Shelf 4	$2.25

Miscellaneous Items	
Seed packets	50¢ or 4 for $1.75
Fertilizer	$5.00
Gloves	$4.50
Cultivators	$2.00
Plant markers	2 for 15¢ or 7 for 40¢
Rake	$19.00
Pots	$12.75
Sun hat	$2.00

1 Kevin bought 2 plant markers, a seed packet, and a sun hat. How much did Kevin spend?
A   65¢
B   67¢
C $7.15
D   Not given

2 Toby bought 3 plants from shelf 2 and 2 plants from shelf 3. Shannon only bought 4 plants, but her total bill was as much as Toby's. From which of the shelves could Shannon have gotten her plant?
J   All 4 plants came from shelf 2.
K   All 4 plants came from shelf 4.
L   Three plants came from shelf 2 and one plant from shelf 1.
M   We cannot tell from where Shannon's plants came.

3 Malik bought 4 seed packets. How much more did he spend than if he had only bought 3 seed packets.
A   25¢
B   50¢
C   75¢
D $1.75

4 Emma spent $6.00 on cultivators and $15.00 on plants. What do you need to know to figure out how many items she bought?
J   She spent $21.00 in all.
K   She bought 3 cultivators.
L   She bought 2 plants from shelf 4.
M   All of the plants were from shelf 3.

GO ➡

Answer rows   A Ⓐ Ⓑ Ⓒ Ⓓ   B Ⓙ Ⓚ Ⓛ Ⓜ   1 Ⓐ Ⓑ Ⓒ Ⓓ   2 Ⓙ Ⓚ Ⓛ Ⓜ   3 Ⓐ Ⓑ Ⓒ Ⓓ   4 Ⓙ Ⓚ Ⓛ Ⓜ

5 Mary bought 30 plant markers. How can she figure out how much she should pay?

  A Multiply 2 times 40¢ then multiply 16 times 15¢ and then add the results together.

  B Multiply 4 times 40¢ and then add 15¢.

  C Multiply 15 times 15¢.

  D Multiply 30 times 15¢.

6 Lila wants to take a painting class that costs $75. She got $50 from her grandmother for her birthday, but she only has $30 left. How much more money does Lila need to pay for the painting class?

  J $20

  K $25

  L $45

  M Not given

7 One week, Lila earned $10 mowing a neighbor's lawn, half that much walking her uncle's dog, and $7 cleaning the garage. How much did she earn that week from these 3 jobs?

  A $17

  B $22

  C $37

  D Not given

8 When she had earned enough money, Lila signed up for the painting class. She decided to buy a paintbrush for $6 and paper for twice as much as the paintbrush. She also paid for the paints which were twice as much as the paper. What else does Lila need to know to figure out how much she spent?

  J The cost of the paper

  K The cost of the paints

  L The cost of the paintbrush and the paper

  M Lila needs to know nothing else

9 After her class was over, Lila decided that she wanted to purchase some more colors of paint. She has $23.47 to spend, and each tube of paint costs $1.89. A good estimate of how many tubes of paint she can buy is given by

  A multiplying 24 times 2.

  B subtracting 2 from 24.

  C dividing 24 by 2.

  D adding 24 and 2.

10 For each bag of cat food Mr. Howell buys, he buys 2 bags of dog food. If he buys 3 bags of cat food, how many bags of animal food will he buy in all?

  A 5

  B 6

  C 9

  D 12

11 A bike rider averages 19 miles an hour. The race is 76 miles long. How can you find out how long it will take the rider to finish the race?

  J Divide 19 into 76.

  K Add 19 and 76.

  L Subtract 19 from 76.

  M Multiply 19 by 76.

GO

Directions: Use the graph below to answer questions 12–14.

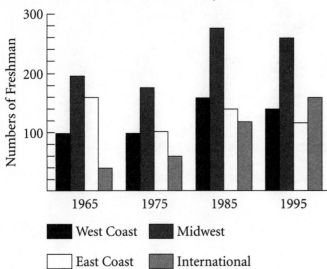

Regional Composition of Freshman Students at Schaalman University 1965-1995

Legend: ■ West Coast ■ Midwest □ East Coast ▨ International

12 In which year was the freshman class the smallest?
J   1965
K   1975
L   1985
M   1995

13 If you asked a freshman at Schaalman University what region she was from, which region would you be most likely to hear?
A   West Coast
B   Midwest
C   East Coast
D   International

14 Which region has never shown decreased counts for the years shown?
J   West Coast
K   Midwest
L   East Coast
M   International

Directions: Use the graph below to answer questions 15–17.

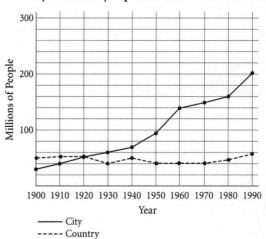

City and country Population in the U.S. 1900-1990

—— City
----- Country

15 In 1950, about how many people were living in cities in the United States?
A   100,000,000
B   10,000,000
C   1,000,000
D   100,000

16 During which of the following decades did the number of people living in cities change the least?
J   1910–1920
K   1920–1930
L   1930–1940
M   1940–1950

17 About how many years did it take for the number of people in cities to double from what it was in 1900?
A   5
B   10
C   20
D   50

STOP

Math Computation

Lesson 12a **Computation**

Directions: Solve each problem. Choose the answer you think is correct. If the correct answer is not given, fill in the space for the last answer, N.

| sample A | 111 − 22 | A 89 B 99 C 133 D N | sample B | 144 + 6 | J 130 K 138 L 140 M N |

TIPS

- Look at the numbers and the operation sign carefully.
- Work the problem on scratch paper before you look at the answer choices.

1 2496
  + 327

A 2,169
B 2,823
C 2,833
D N

2 3000
  × 90

J 270,000
K 300,009
L 300,900
M N

3 8)7326

A 914
B 914 R6
C 915 R6
D N

4 0.094 − 0.07 =

J 0.0024
K 0.087
L 0.164
M N

5 $\frac{10}{15}$
  − $\frac{4}{15}$

A $\frac{1}{6}$
B $\frac{2}{5}$
C $\frac{14}{15}$
D N

6 $\frac{1}{12} + \frac{7}{12} + \frac{1}{12} =$

J $\frac{1}{2}$
K $\frac{2}{3}$
L 1
M N

7 14.2
  9.0
  6.2
  + 2.7

A 29.1
B 32.1
C 32.2
D N

8 0.35 × 6 =

J 2.10
K 21.0
L 210
M N

STOP

Math Computation

Lesson 12b **Computation**

Directions: Solve each problem. Choose the answer you think is correct. If the correct answer is not given, fill in the space for the last answer, N.

| Sample A | $\frac{2}{8}$ $-\frac{1}{4}$ | A 0
 B $\frac{1}{4}$
 C $\frac{1}{2}$
 D N | Sample B | 88
 10
 36
 + 54 | J 168
 K 188
 L 190
 M N |

- **Set the problem up carefully on scratch paper. Align numbers and decimal points correctly.**

1 $77 \div 10 =$
  A 67
  B 77.10
  C 770
  D N

2 0.401
  − 0.308
  J 0.0093
  K 0.0903
  L 0.093
  M N

3 $\frac{1}{9} \times 3 =$
  A $\frac{1}{3}$
  B 27
  C 3
  D N

4 309
  × 20
  J 329
  K 5,180
  L 6,108
  M N

5 $230 - 51 =$
  A 221
  B 179
  C 281
  D N

6 $33\overline{)400}$
  J 11 R10
  K 12 R3
  L 12 R4
  M N

7 $0.0102 + 0.304 =$
  A 0.03142
  B 0.3142
  C 0.3412
  D N

8 $\frac{1}{4} \times \frac{1}{6} =$
  J $\frac{1}{24}$
  K $\frac{1}{10}$
  L $\frac{2}{3}$
  M N

STOP

Answer rows A Ⓐ Ⓑ Ⓒ Ⓓ   1 Ⓐ Ⓑ Ⓒ Ⓓ   3 Ⓐ Ⓑ Ⓒ Ⓓ   5 Ⓐ Ⓑ Ⓒ Ⓓ   7 Ⓐ Ⓑ Ⓒ Ⓓ
B Ⓙ Ⓚ Ⓛ Ⓜ   2 Ⓙ Ⓚ Ⓛ Ⓜ   4 Ⓙ Ⓚ Ⓛ Ⓜ   6 Ⓙ Ⓚ Ⓛ Ⓜ   8 Ⓙ Ⓚ Ⓛ Ⓜ

Math Computation

Lesson 13a **Computation**

Directions: Solve each problem. Choose the answer you think is correct. If the correct answer is not given, fill in the space for the last answer, N.

Sample A $0.64 - 0.58 =$

- A 0.06
- B 0.6
- C 6
- D N

Sample B $\frac{7}{12} - \frac{5}{12} =$

- J $\frac{1}{6}$
- K $\frac{1}{4}$
- L $\frac{2}{24}$
- M N

- • If the answer you find is not one of the choices, work the problem again.
- • Rewrite horizontal problems so you can solve them.

1
$$\begin{array}{r} 6385 \\ + 307 \end{array}$$
- A 6,592
- B 6,692
- C 7,782
- D N

2 $945 \div 35 =$
- J 31 R5
- K 27
- L 270
- M N

3
$$\begin{array}{r} 25 \\ 37 \\ 59 \\ + 68 \end{array}$$
- A 174
- B 179
- C 189
- D N

4 $\frac{1}{9} + \frac{4}{9} =$
- J $\frac{5}{81}$
- K $\frac{5}{18}$
- L $\frac{5}{9}$
- M N

5
$$\begin{array}{r} 623 \\ - 276 \end{array}$$
- A 453
- B 447
- C 457
- D N

6
$$\begin{array}{r} 804 \\ \times 50 \end{array}$$
- J 4,020
- K 4,200
- L 40,200
- M N

7 $\frac{3}{4} + \frac{1}{4} =$
- A 1
- B $\frac{3}{4}$
- C $\frac{1}{2}$
- D N

8 $\frac{7}{8} - \frac{2}{8} =$
- J $\frac{5}{8}$
- K $\frac{5}{16}$
- L 5
- M N

STOP

Math Computation

Unit 8

Lesson 13b **Computation**

Directions: Solve each problem. Choose the answer you think is correct. If the correct answer is not given, fill in the space for the last answer, N.

Sample A	$40 \times 900 =$	A	360
		B	3,600
		C	36,000
		D	N

Sample B	0.21	J	0.84
	$\times\ 4$	K	8.4
		L	84
		M	N

- **Estimate the size of your answer. Eliminate answer choices that are too large or too small.**

1 $\frac{2}{18} + \frac{1}{18} =$

A $\frac{1}{18}$

B $\frac{3}{36}$

C $\frac{3}{18}$

D N

2 303
$\times 300$

J 9,090
K 90,900
L 99,000
M N

3 $842 - 375 =$

A 473
B 533
C 567
D N

4 $\frac{3}{7} \times 5 =$

J $\frac{3}{35}$

K $2\frac{1}{7}$

L $5\frac{3}{7}$

M N

5 0.14
0.93
$+ 0.71$

A 0.178
B 1.78
C)1.88
D N

6 $6\overline{)228}$

J 21 R2
K 31 R2
L 38
M N

7 302
$\times\ 30$

A 9,060
B 9,600
C 30,230
D N

8 8625
$-\ 3471$

J 5,154
K 5,244
L 12,096
M N

STOP

Answer rows   A Ⓐ Ⓑ Ⓒ Ⓓ   **1** Ⓐ Ⓑ Ⓒ Ⓓ   **3** Ⓐ Ⓑ Ⓒ Ⓓ   **5** Ⓐ Ⓑ Ⓒ Ⓓ   **7** Ⓐ Ⓑ Ⓒ Ⓓ
                  B Ⓙ Ⓚ Ⓛ Ⓜ   **2** Ⓙ Ⓚ Ⓛ Ⓜ   **4** Ⓙ Ⓚ Ⓛ Ⓜ   **6** Ⓙ Ⓚ Ⓛ Ⓜ   **8** Ⓙ Ⓚ Ⓛ Ⓜ

65

Test Yourself: Math Computation

Unit 8

Directions: Solve each problem. Choose the answer you think is correct. If the correct answer is not given, fill in the space for the last answer, N.

Sample A	$827 - 689$	A	38
		B	118
		C	138
		D	N

Sample B	$0.6 + 0.1 =$	J	0.07
		K	0.7
		L	6.1
		M	N

1 $\frac{5}{7} + \frac{2}{7} =$

A $\frac{3}{7}$

B $\frac{5}{7}$

C 1

D N

2
```
   72
   50
   14
 + 36
```
J 172
K 174
L 182
M N

3 $47 \times 40 =$

A 1,680
B 1,780
C 1,860
D N

4
```
  722
− 246
```
J 424
K 476
L 968
M N

5
```
   7.54
 + 9.79
```
A 16.33
B 17.33
C 18.32
D N

6 $432 \div 8 =$

J 54
K 54 R2
L 55 R4
M N

7 $31\overline{)947}$

A 29 R7
B 30 R7
C 31
D N

8 $21 \times 5000 =$

J 1,050
K 10,500
L 105,000
M N

GO

9 $\frac{7}{9}$

  $-\ \frac{1}{6}$

A $\frac{6}{18}$

B $\frac{11}{18}$

C 3

D N

10 $4740 \times 25 =$

J 1,185

K 11,850

L 118,500

M N

11 $0.7 \times 0.3 =$

A 0.21

B 2.1

C 21

D N

12 $\frac{8}{9} - \frac{5}{9} =$

J $\frac{1}{3}$

K $\frac{1}{18}$

L 3

M N

13   45

  $\times\ 16$

A 315

B 710

C 720

D N

14 $3.7 + 0.269 =$

J 0.3060

K 0.639

L 3.969

M N

15 $\frac{1}{3} \times \frac{7}{6} =$

A $\frac{1}{36}$

B $\frac{1}{9}$

C $\frac{7}{18}$

D N

16 $6\overline{)45} =$

J 7.4

K 7.5

L 70

M N

17   0.16

  $\times\ 0.04$

A 0.064

B 0.64

C 6.4

D N

18 $\frac{1}{9} + \frac{5}{6} =$

J $\frac{1}{12}$

K $\frac{6}{15}$

L $\frac{17}{18}$

M N

STOP

Maps, Diagrams, and Reference Materials

Lesson 14a **Maps and Diagrams**

Sample A	ROOM	8:00	9:00	10:00	11:00	12:00
	101	Math.	Math.	Sci.	Sci.	Sci.
	102	Eng.	Eng.	Eng.	Hist.	Hist.
	103	Comp.	Comp.	Comp.	Comp.	Comp.
	104	Art	Art	Art	Art	Art
	105	Geo.	Geo.	Geo.	Econ.	Econ.

Which class will be held at 11:00 in room 102?

A Science
B History
C Composition
D Art

- If a question has a map or graphic, be sure you look at it carefully before you choose your answer.

- Skip difficult items and return to them later, if you have time.

Directions: This diagram shows an unfolded box. Use the diagram to answer questions 1–3.

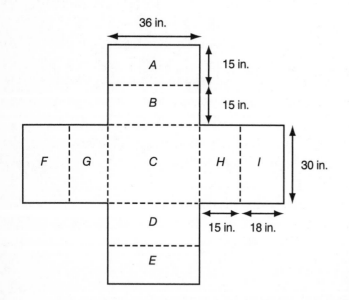

1 What are the dimensions of the box?
A 36 in. long × 33 in. wide × 30 in. deep
B 36 in. long × 30 in. wide × 33 in. deep
C 30 in. long × 30 in. wide × 15 in. deep
D 36 in. long × 30 in. wide × 15 in. deep

2 If you assembled the box, which pieces might form the top?
J *A* and *E*
K *B* and *D*
L *G* and *H*
M *G*, *C*, and *H*

3 To assemble the box, what should you do first?
A Tape pieces *A* and *E* together
B Fold up sides *B*, *G*, *H*, and *D*
C Fold sides *H* and *I* over *C*
D Tape pieces *F* and *G* together

GO

Directions: The map below shows a make-believe region of the United States. Use the map to answer questions 4–8.

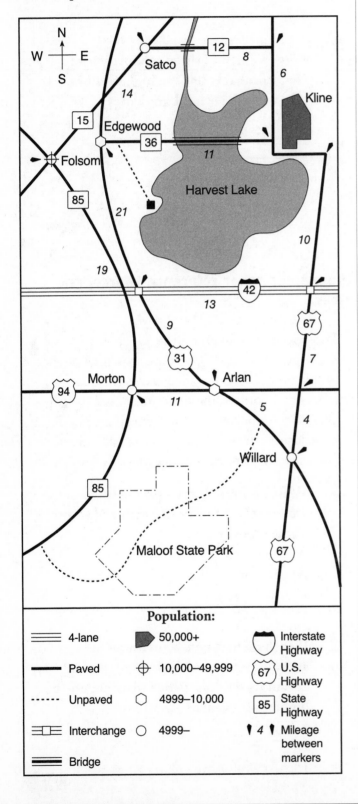

4 What is the mileage between Edgewood and Arlan?

J 9 miles
K 21 miles
L 28 miles
M 30 miles

5 Which of these towns might have a population of 43,519?

A Folsom
B Morton
C Willard
D Satco

6 A family is driving east from Edgewood. What would they come upon before they reached Kline?

J A very short bridge
K A very long bridge
L A state park
M The town of Folsom

7 If a family went to Maloof State Park, they would have to

A drive on unpaved roads.
B visit Edgewood first.
C park their car at Morton and hike in.
D travel on Route 15.

8 Which of these highways goes from southwest to northeast?

J Interstate Highway 42
K State Highway 15
L State Highway 85
M U.S. Highway 94

STOP

Unit 9

Maps, Diagrams, and Reference Materials

Lesson 14b Maps and Diagrams

Directions: Use the maps below to answer the questions.

Sample A About how many kilometers is the most direct trip from the Tokay District Office to the Dekum District Office?

A 10
B 50
C 100
D 150

Sample B Which of these school districts probably has the highest number of middle school graduates?

J Tokay
K Ketchum
L Lodi
M O'Mally

• Read the questions, check the map or other reference source, and then look at the answer choices.

Map of County School Districts

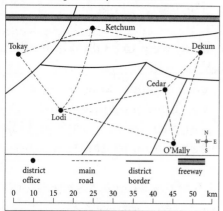

Number of Students in Each District

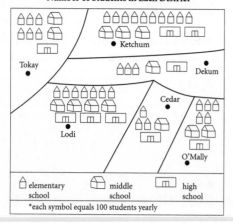

Directions: The maps on the left show a make-believe county. There are six school districts in this county. The top map shows the district offices and borders, the main roads, and the freeway. The bottom map shows the elementary, middle, and high school student populations of each district. Use these maps to answer questions 1–4.

1 Which school district probably has students that live both north and south of the freeway?

A O'Mally
B Cedar
C Dekum
D Ketchum

2 If each district gets a government allowance based on how many students attend its schools, which district gets the highest allowance?

J Tokay
K Lodi
L Ketchum
M Dekum

GO

Lesson 14b **Maps and Diagrams**

3 What school district is northwest of Cedar School District?

A Tokay
B Lodi
C Dekum
D O'Mally

4 In which direction does the freeway run?

J North and west
K North and south
L East and west
M East and south

Directions: A group of students studying consumer economics compared Candid brand cameras. This is a chart of their findings. Use it to answer questions 5–10.

Candid Cameras

	Model	Price	Style	Auto Focus	Flash	Accessories
A Series	A1-10	$$	35 mm			batteries
	A1-50	$$	35 mm			batteries, tripod
	A1-80	$$$	digital	✓		filters, batteries, tripod
B Series	B2-10	$	35 mm	✓	✓	batteries
	B2-20	$	35 mm	✓	✓	filters
	B2-30	$$	digital	✓		batteries, tripod
C Series	C3-12	$	35 mm		✓	filters
	C3-18	$	35 mm		✓	filters
	C3-21	$$	35 mm			filters, batteries, tripod
	C3-28	$$$	digital	✓		filters, batteries, tripod

Key: $ = 0-200   ○ filters
         $$ = 201-400   ▯▯ batteries
         $$$ = 401-900   ⋀ tripod

5 Which camera model might sell for $150?

A A1-10
B A1-50
C B2-10
D C3-28

6 Which of these accessories comes with all of the cameras in the A1 series?

J Batteries
K Filters
L Tripods
M Film

7 For which camera would you not have to buy filters?

A A1-10
B A1-50
C B2-20
D B2-30

8 Which camera would be most useful if you didn't want to buy film?

J B2-10
K C3-12
L C3-21
M C3-28

9 The C3-28 model probably costs more than the C3-21 model because

A the C3-28 comes with more accessories.
B the C3-28 is a digital camera.
C the C3-28 is part of a more expensive series.
D the C3-28 is an older, time-tested model.

10 If Claudia wants a camera that she can set up to take pictures of herself with others, which of these would be the least expensive camera that meets her needs?

J A1-50
K B2-10
L C3-18
M C3-28

Answer rows   **3** Ⓐ Ⓑ Ⓒ Ⓓ   **5** Ⓐ Ⓑ Ⓒ Ⓓ   **7** Ⓐ Ⓑ Ⓒ Ⓓ   **9** Ⓐ Ⓑ Ⓒ Ⓓ
                          4 Ⓙ Ⓚ Ⓛ Ⓜ   **6** Ⓙ Ⓚ Ⓛ Ⓜ   **8** Ⓙ Ⓚ Ⓛ Ⓜ   **10** Ⓙ Ⓚ Ⓛ Ⓜ

71

Unit 9 Maps, Diagrams, and Reference Materials

Lesson 15a **Reference Materials**

Sample A

INDEX

Electricity, 278–309, 370; batteries, 288–289, 370; circuits, 287; current, 279; generator, 304–305; solar cell, 291; static, 278, 281; wind turbine, 39

On which page would you find information about static electricity?

A 305
B 291
C 278
D 282

- Skim the reference source then answer the questions. Look back at the reference source to find the answers.

- Think carefully about what the question is asking before you choose an answer.

Directions: Questions 1–6 are about using library materials. Choose the best answer for each question.

1 What would you find in an atlas?
A How to pronounce the word Zimbabwe
B A map of Zimbabwe
C The history of Zimbabwe
D How to use Zimbabwe in a sentence

2 Which section of a textbook would define the special words used in the book?
J The index
K The table of contents
L The glossary
M The bibliography

3 In which section of the library would you find a world atlas?
A Periodicals
B Nonfiction
C Fiction
D Reference

4 Which key term should you use to learn about the desert plants found in America, Asia and Africa?
J Plant
K Asia
L Desert
M Africa

5 Which of these would most likely be discussed in a geography book?
A The development of the Chinese language
B Chinese imports into the United States
C The boundary between China and Korea
D The government of China

6 Which of these would you find in an encyclopedia?
J Information about the Mason-Dixon line
K The pronunciation of the word *hale*
L A synonym for the word *persistence*
M Information about the mayor of Dallas

STOP

mace (mās), n. a spice ground from nutmeg.

ma·chine (mə **shēn'**), n., 1.a mechanical apparatus used to perform work. v. 2.to create something with a machine.

mac·u·la (**mak' yə** lə), n., pl. **maculae.** maculae. a spot or blotch on the skin.

mad·r·igal (**mad'ri** gəl), n. a lyric poem that ca be set to music.

mag·a·zine (**mag' ə** zēn', mag' ə **zēn'**), n. 1.a publication that is issued periodically. 2.a room or place for keeping explosives.

mag·ni·fy (**mag'nə** fī'), v. to increase the apparent size through a lens. 2.to increase the size of. 3.to make more exciting or intense.

main·tain (mān **tāw'**), v.t. to keep in existence. 2.to keep in good condition.

maize (māz), n.1. corn. 2. a pale yellow color.

ma·jor (**mā'** jər), n.1. a commissioned officer in the military above captain. adj.2. great in size, amount, or importance.

Pronunciation Guide for this dictionary:

a rat	i bit	u nut	ə stands for
ā lay	ī tie	û burn	a in metal
ě net	ǒ not		o in lemon
e me	o so		

Direction: Use the dictionary sample above to answer questions 7–12.

7 **Maize is**
  A   a kind of animal.
  B   a type of food plant.
  C   an English recipe.
  D   a dark color.

8 **The i in machine sounds like the**
  J   *e* in let.
  K   *e* in me.
  L   *i* in lie.
  M   *a* in day.

9 **Which word fits best in the sentence: If you own an automobile, it is important that you _____ it well?**
  A   maintain   C   major
  B   machine   D   mace

10 **What is the plural of macula?**
  J   maculies   L   maculaies
  K   maculas   M   maculae

11 **How are the two pronunciations of *magazine* different?**
  A   The number of syllables is different.
  B   The letter a is pronounced differently.
  C   The accent is on different syllables.
  D   They have different plural forms.

12 **How do you spell the word that means a poem that can be set to music?**
  J   Madregal
  K   Madregel
  L   Medrigal
  M   Madrigal

STOP

Unit 9

Maps, Diagrams, and Reference Materials

Lesson 15b Reference Materials

Directions: Use the index below to answer the questions.

Sample A

INDEX

Electricity, 278-309, 370; batteries, 288-289, 370; circuits, 287; current, 279; generator, 304-305; solar cell, 291; static, 278, 281; wind turbine, 39

Frequency modulation (FM), 254, 255

Which page would tell you about electricity using a wind turbine?
A   39
B   278
C   291
D   305

- **Look for key words in the question. They will tell you where to look in the map or other reference source.**

- **Remember, the correct answers in this lesson can always be found in the reference source.**

INDEX

Aircraft, 118–119; artificial horizon, 81; autopilot, 311, 313; flight, 114, 116–117; history, 362; jet engine, 168-170

Automobile, 445–456; automatic trans-mission, 326–327; battery, 289; brakes, 90; carburetor, 148; cruise control, 329; speed-ometer, 50; windshield wiper, 53

Camera, 367; color photography, 214–215; electronic flash, 192; film, 210–211; instant, 216, 367; television, 258–259

Car., *See* Automobile

da Vinci, Leonardo, 361–362

Electricity, 278-309, 370; batteries, 288–289, 370; circuits, 287; current, 279; generator, 304–305; solar cell, 291; static, 278, 281; wind turbine, 39

Gravity, and flight, 115; gyroscope, 80–81; parachute, 87

Internal combustion engine, 164, 360

Laser, 206–208; compact disk, 243, 248–249; printer, 348–349; supermarket checkout, 350

Directions: The index on the left is from a book called *Physics in Everyday Life.* Use the index to answer questions 1–4.

1 Which page would discuss how lasers are used to make compact discs?
A   206   C   248
B   208   D   348

2 Which page would tell you about the autopilot on an aircraft?
J   118   L   311
K   168   M   314

3 Which page would explain how electricity can be generated by a wind turbine?
A   87   C   399
B   281   D   499

4 Which page would discuss the inventions of Leonardo da Vinci?
J   118   L   287
K   127   M   361

STOP

Lesson 16a Reference Materials

Sample A
Electricity, 278–309, 370; batteries, 288–289, 370; circuits, 287; current, 279; generator, 304–305; solar cell, 291; static, 278, 281; wind turbine, 39

On which page would you find information about static electricity?
A   305
B   291
C   278
D   282

- Look at the reference source carefully. Don't be confused by all the information it contains.

Directions: Use this card from a library card catalog to do Questions 1–4.

COMPUTER REPAIR

622   Fair, Ann R.
G443   *If It's Broken, Fix It* / by Ann R. Fair; photos and drawings by Louis Abbruzzo.
    -San Francisco, CA: Technology Press, 1995
    320 p.: photos; 23 cm.
1. Computers. 2. Electronics. 3. Appliance Repair. I. Abbruzzo, Louis II. Title.

1   What is the title of this book?
A   *Computer Repair*
B   *If It's Broken, Fix It*
C   *Technology*
D   *Electronics*

2   According to this catalog card, where might you find other books about computer repair?
J   Electricity
K   Home Repairs
L   Photos
M   Electronics

3   What kind of catalog entry is this?
A   An author listing
B   A title listing
C   A subject listing
D   A publisher listing

4   Who is Ann R. Fair?
J   The publisher of the book
K   The photographer for the book
L   The printer of the book
M   The author of the book

GO ➡

Directions: Questions 5–11 are about library materials. Choose the best answer for each question.

5 **Which of these would tell you the meaning of the word *pontificate*?**

A   An almanac
B   A dictionary
C   An encyclopedia
D   A science book

6 **Which of these would tell you when Antarctica was first explored?**

J   A dictionary
K   A science book
L   A geography book
M   An encyclopedia

7 **Which of these would tell you what countries are in the continent of South America?**

A   A map of the United States
B   A dictionary
C   A world atlas
D   A book about the South

8 **Which of these magazines would most likely have an article about how to repair broken automatic windows?**

J   Old Cars Weekly
K   Inside Automotives
L   The Trucker
M   New England Mechanic

9 **In which section of the library would you find an encyclopedia?**

A   Literature
B   Reference
C   Geography
D   Periodicals

10 **Which of these would you find in the index of a book about presidents of the United States?**

J   A list the chapters and what pages they begin on
K   An alphabetical list of words and their definitions
L   A list of pages with information about Abraham Lincoln
M   The titles of other books about United States presidents

11 **Which of these would contain a list of the planets in the universe?**

A   A collection of maps
B   A weather book
C   A space science book
D   A science fiction book

STOP

Maps, Diagrams, and Reference Materials

Lesson 16b **Reference Materials**

Directions: Use the dictionary entry below to answer the questions.

Sample A How should you spell the name of a type of fabric?
A   Gosamer
B   Gossamer
C   Gosammer
D   Gosamere

Sample B How do the two pronunciations of *gourmand* differ?
J   The *g* is pronounced differently.
K   The *ou* is pronounced differently.
L   The *r* is silent in one and not the other.
M   The accent is on different syllables.

• **Take your best guess when unsure of the answer.**

Directions: Use this sample from a dictionary page to answer questions 1–3.

---

gla · cial (**glā'** shəl), adj. 1. having to do with glaciers or ice sheets. 2. moving extremely slowly.

gos · sa · mer (**gos'ə** mər), n. 1. a fine, filmy cobweb. 2. a thin, light fabric.

gour · mand (gŏŏr' **mänd'**, gŏŏr' mənd), n. a person who is fond of eating.

gulch (gulch), n., **gulches,** n.pl. a narrow ravine, often marking the course of a stream.

gul · li · ble (**gul'ə** bəl), adj. easily deceived; trusting.

Pronunciation Guide for this dictionary:

a rat	i bit	u nut	ə stands for
ā lay	ī tie	û burn	a in metal
ä calm	ŏ not	ŏŏ look	o in lemon
ĕ net	o so		
e me			

---

1 What is the plural of gulch?
A   Gulches
B   Gulchs
C   Gulchies
D   Gulchses

2 What word best completes the sentence "I never should have believed what the advertisement said. I was far too _____"?
J   Gulch
K   Gullible
L   Glacial
M   Gossamer

3 In which sentence is the second meaning of the word glacial used correctly?
A   From our ship we could see the glacial landscape.
B   My fingers were glacial so I put on some gloves.
C   The line in front of the restaurant moved at a glacial pace.
D   It was nice and glacial outside, so we decided to go skiing.

Answer rows
A Ⓐ Ⓑ Ⓒ Ⓓ   1 Ⓐ Ⓑ Ⓒ Ⓓ   3 Ⓐ Ⓑ Ⓒ Ⓓ
B Ⓙ Ⓚ Ⓛ Ⓜ   2 Ⓙ Ⓚ Ⓛ Ⓜ

Sample A

INDEX

Electricity, 278–309, 370; batteries, 288–289, 370; circuits, 287; current, 279; generator, 304–305; solar cell, 291; static, 278, 281; wind turbine, 39

Frequency modulation (FM), 254, 255

Which page would discuss how to generate electric power using a solar cell?

A 278
B 287
C 291
D 304

Directions: Josie and her dad found these "Make your own bookshelf" diagrams in a woodworking magazine. The numbers show inches and the dotted lines show where the wood should be cut. Use the diagrams to answer questions 1–6.

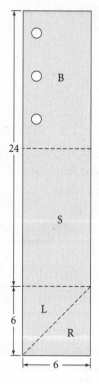

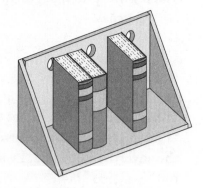

1 Which of these would be the first step in putting the bookshelf together?
A Nailing piece B to piece S
B Cutting the wood into four pieces
C Measuring and marking the wood
D Drilling the holes in piece B

2 Which part of the bookshelf is piece S?
J The left side
K The right side
L The back
M The bottom

3 What is the purpose of the three holes in piece B?
A To use as bookshelf dividers
B To use to hang the bookshelf
C To make the bookshelf stronger
D To make the bookshelf easy to carry

4 When the bookshelf is assembled, which two pieces are attached to every other piece?
J Pieces B and S
K Pieces B and L
L Pieces R and B
M Pieces L and R

5 Which piece of wood would be just big enough to make three of these bookshelves?
A 6" × 30"
B 6" × 75"
C 6" × 90"
D 6" × 100"

6 How deep is the assembled bookshelf from front to back?
J 6"
K 12"
L 24"
M 30

Directions: The map below is part of a larger, road map. Use this map to answer questions 7–11.

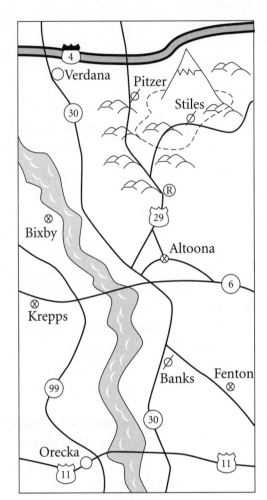

Population:

▌ Major hwy	○ 25,000	🛡4 interstate hwy
│ two lane road	∅ 10,000-24,999	⑳29 US hwy
┆ gravel road	⊗ 1,000-9,999	⑨99 state hwy
⊢—⊣ 5 miles		⌒⌒ mountains
		® rest stop

7 When traveling from Orecka to Altoona, what kind of roads will you spend most of your time on?

A   Interstate highways
B   U.S. highways
C   State highways
D   Two-lane roads

8 About how many miles shorter was the trip from Orecka to Banks when U.S. Highway 11 was built?

J   10
K   50
L   100
M   150

9 Which of these towns would probably have the most tourist attractions?

A   Fenton
B   Bixby
C   Verdana
D   Stiles

10 If you took the shortest route, what would be the distance from Verdana to Pitzer?

J   About 20 miles
K   About 50 miles
L   About 100 miles
M   About 125 miles

11 Along which highway would you most likely see a sign for Bixby?

J   Interstate 4
K   U.S. Highway 29
L   State Highway 99
M   State Highway 30

GO

Directions: The map below shows part of a state park. Use this map to answer questions 12–16.

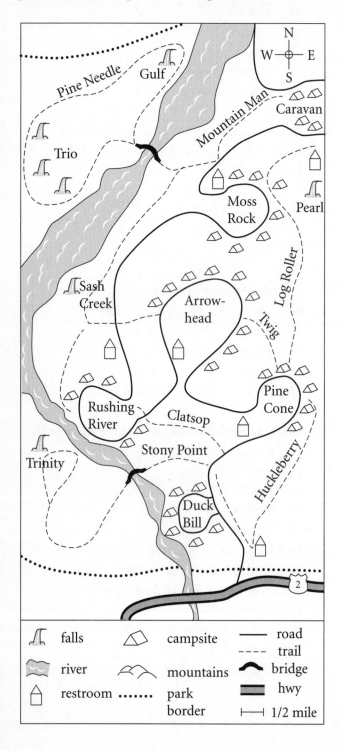

12 In going from the Duck Bill campsite to the Rushing River campsite by the shortest route, which would you follow?
J   The campsite road
K   The park border
L   A state highway
M   Campsite trails

13 About how many miles is it from the park's south entrance to the Pine Cone campsite?
A   1

B   3

C   5

D   7

14 Which of these campsites would most likely have direct access to the river's sandy beaches?
J   Caravan
K   Moss Rock
L   Duck Bill
M   Arrowhead

15 Using the shortest route, about how far is the distance between the Pine Cone and Moss Rock campsites?
A   2 miles
B   4 miles
C   8 miles
D   16 miles

16 Along which trail would you most likely see a sign for Trinity Falls?
J   Stony Point
K   Log Roller
L   Sash Creek
M   Pine Needle

GO

caus·tic (kô' stik), adj. 1. capable of burning or destroying living tissue. 2. severely critical or sarcastic.

cav·a·lier (kav'ə lēr', kav'ə ler'), n., adj. 1.a horseman, especially a mounted soldier; knight. 2. one having the spirit or bearing of a knight; gallant.

chaff (chaff), n. the husks of grain and grasses that are separated during threshing.

chap·ar·ral (shap'ə ral'), n. a dense growth of shrubs or small trees.

cha·ris·ma (kə riz' mə), n. a spiritual power or personal quality that gives an individual power over people.

cheeky (chē' kē), adj. impudent; rude, or bold.

con·done (kən dōn'), v.t. to give unspoken approval by overlooking something that is illegal or wrong.

cov·en·ant (kəv'ə nənt), n. an agreement, usually formal, between two parties, to do or not do something specific.

cu·li·na·ry (kyōo'lə nev'ē, kul' ə) adj. of, or pertaining to, or used in cooking or the kitchen.

Pronunciation Guide for this dictionary:

a rat	i bit	u nut	ə stands for
ā lay	ī tie	û burn	a in metal
ä calm	ŏ not	ŏŏ look	o in lemon
ĕ net	o so	ô ball	
e me			

17 **How do the two pronunciations of *cavalier* differ?**
A The *c* is pronounced differently.
B The a is pronounced differently.
C The *ier* is pronounced differently.
D The accent is on different syllables.

18 **What is the plural of covenant?**
J Covenent
K Covenants
L Covenantes
M Covenantses

19 **Which word fits best in the sentence: Joey's _____ personality attracts people to him.**
A charismatic
B charisma
C charismatize
D charismas

20 **Which word fits best in this sentence: By choosing to ignore her son's rude behavior, she was actually _____ it.**
J condone
K condoning
L condoner
M condonable

21 **In which sentence is a form of the word caustic used correctly?**
A The rope broke almost instantly; it was not caustic at all.
B The bully's caustic retort hurt several people's feelings.
C The campfire was perfectly caustic for keeping us warm.
D The tickets were not caustic; they were cheaper than I expected.

Directions: At the top of each page in a dictionary, there are two guide words. They are the first and last words on that page of the dictionary. Use the guide words and page numbers below to answer questions 22–26.

branch	•	bravo	205
brawl	•	break	206
breakable	•	breathless	207
breathy	•	brevity	208
brew	•	briefing	209

22 On which page would you find the word **bray**?

J   206
K   207
L   208
M   209

23 On which page would you find the word **breeze**?

A   205
B   206
C   207
D   208

24 On which page would you find the word **brand**?

J   205
K   206
L   207
M   208

25 On which page would you find the word **bride**?

A   205
B   206
C   207
D   209

26 On which page would you find the word **brick**?

J   206
K   207
L   208
M   209

Directions: Before you use some reference sources, you must decide which word or phrase to use to find the information you want. This word or phrase is called the key term. For questions 27–31, select the key term.

27 Which key term should you use to learn about the Rio Grande, a river that establishes the border between the United States and Mexico?

A   Rio Grande   C   United States
B   River   D   Mexico

28 Which key term should you use to find out the most about the Olympic sport of decathlon in which one person does ten track and field events?

J   Sport   L   Decathlon
K   Track and Field   M   Olympics

29 Which key term should you use to find the diameter of the planet Mars?

A   Diameter   C   Planet
B   Mars   D   Size

30 Death Valley is an unusual desert region in the West. Which key term should you use to find out where it is located?

J   Death Valley   L   Region
K   Desert   M   West

31 In Canada, one of the national holidays is called Dominion Day. Which key term should you use to find out what this holiday celebrates?

A   Holiday   C   Canada
B   National   D   Dominion
                          Day

GO

Directions: This is part of an index from a book called *The Kids' Summer Handbook.* Use it to answer questions 32–37.

B
beach. see sand
berries, 19; 140–142
black flies, 139
boats, 20; anchor, 47; bailer, 48;
    balloon-powered, 22; balsam races, 23;
    cardboard, 20–21; key float, 46;
    origami, 166–167; safety, 49
bonfire. see campfire
C
camping, 144–151
campfire, 113; cooking, 117; siting, 114–115;
    songs, 119; starting, 116; stories, 118
canoes, 42; accessories, 43; cardboard, 20–21;
    strokes, 44–45; tips, 43
card games, 165
cooking, meals, 117; snacks 144–145, 178–179
D
diving raft, 40–41
dried fruit, 140, 178–179
G
games, playing card, 165; rainy-day, 164–165
    swimming, 32–35
I
ice pops, 18
insect repellant, 135, 139
insects, 19, 26–27, 59, 77, 94–95, 120, 139, 150
    water, 26-27, 51
S
smores, 144
swimming, games, 32–35; strokes, 36–38
V
vegetable garden, 56–57
W
water, games, 32–35; safety, 30; tricks, 14–15
waterscope, 50–51
weather, forecasting from nature, 158–159;
    predicting, 154–159; recording, 160–161

32 Which page would provide tips on water safety while boating?
J   49
K   30
L   40
M   43

33 Where would you start reading to find out about insects you may encounter while swimming?
A   19
B   26
C   51
D   135

34 Which page would be most likely to tell you how to tell what the weather will be like?
J   155
K   158
L   159
M   160

35 Which page would describe how to select the proper site for a campfire?
A   43
B   113
C   114
D   116

36 Which page would tell what to cook for dinner while camping?
J   18
K   56
L   117
M   178

37 Where would you start reading to find out how to build your own model canoe?
A   42
B   20
C   43
D   166

STOP

Name and Answer Sheet

To the Student:

Now that you have completed the lessons in this book, you are on your way to scoring high!

These tests will give you a chance to put the tips you have learned to work.

A few last reminders …

- Be sure you understand all the directions before you begin each test. You may ask the teacher questions about the directions if you do not understand them.

- Work as quickly as you can during each test.

- When you change an answer, be sure to erase your first mark completely.

- You can guess at an answer or skip difficult items and go back to them later.

- Use the tips you have learned whenever you can.

- It is OK to be a little nervous.

STUDENT'S NAME		SCHOOL

LAST   FIRST   MI

TEACHER

FEMALE ○   MALE ○

BIRTH DATE

MONTH	DAY	YEAR
JAN ○	0 0	0
FEB ○	1 1	1
MAR ○	2 2	2
APR ○	3 3	3
MAY ○	4	4
JUN ○	5	5
JUL ○	6	6
AUG ○	7	7
SEP ○	8	8 8
OCT ○	9	9 9
NOV ○		
DEC ○		

GRADE
⑤   ⑥   ⑦

Book 6

Scoring High

on the

ITBS®

Copyright © 2003 by SRA/McGraw-Hill

TEST 1   VOCABULARY

A Ⓐ Ⓑ Ⓒ Ⓓ	3 Ⓐ Ⓑ Ⓒ Ⓓ	7 Ⓐ Ⓑ Ⓒ Ⓓ	11 Ⓐ Ⓑ Ⓒ Ⓓ	15 Ⓐ Ⓑ Ⓒ Ⓓ
B Ⓙ Ⓚ Ⓛ Ⓜ	4 Ⓙ Ⓚ Ⓛ Ⓜ	8 Ⓙ Ⓚ Ⓛ Ⓜ	12 Ⓙ Ⓚ Ⓛ Ⓜ	16 Ⓙ Ⓚ Ⓛ Ⓜ
1 Ⓐ Ⓑ Ⓒ Ⓓ	5 Ⓐ Ⓑ Ⓒ Ⓓ	9 Ⓐ Ⓑ Ⓒ Ⓓ	13 Ⓐ Ⓑ Ⓒ Ⓓ	17 Ⓐ Ⓑ Ⓒ Ⓓ
2 Ⓙ Ⓚ Ⓛ Ⓜ	6 Ⓙ Ⓚ Ⓛ Ⓜ	10 Ⓙ Ⓚ Ⓛ Ⓜ	14 Ⓙ Ⓚ Ⓛ Ⓜ	18 Ⓙ Ⓚ Ⓛ Ⓜ

TEST 2   READING COMPREHENSION

A Ⓐ Ⓑ Ⓒ Ⓓ	3 Ⓐ Ⓑ Ⓒ Ⓓ	6 Ⓙ Ⓚ Ⓛ Ⓜ	9 Ⓐ Ⓑ Ⓒ Ⓓ	12 Ⓙ Ⓚ Ⓛ Ⓜ	15 Ⓐ Ⓑ Ⓒ Ⓓ
1 Ⓐ Ⓑ Ⓒ Ⓓ	4 Ⓙ Ⓚ Ⓛ Ⓜ	7 Ⓐ Ⓑ Ⓒ Ⓓ	10 Ⓙ Ⓚ Ⓛ Ⓜ	13 Ⓐ Ⓑ Ⓒ Ⓓ	16 Ⓙ Ⓚ Ⓛ Ⓜ
2 Ⓙ Ⓚ Ⓛ Ⓜ	5 Ⓐ Ⓑ Ⓒ Ⓓ	8 Ⓙ Ⓚ Ⓛ Ⓜ	11 Ⓐ Ⓑ Ⓒ Ⓓ	14 Ⓙ Ⓚ Ⓛ Ⓜ	17 Ⓐ Ⓑ Ⓒ Ⓓ

TEST 3   SPELLING

A Ⓐ Ⓑ Ⓒ Ⓓ Ⓔ	1 Ⓐ Ⓑ Ⓒ Ⓓ Ⓔ	3 Ⓐ Ⓑ Ⓒ Ⓓ Ⓔ	5 Ⓐ Ⓑ Ⓒ Ⓓ Ⓔ	7 Ⓐ Ⓑ Ⓒ Ⓓ Ⓔ	9 Ⓐ Ⓑ Ⓒ Ⓓ Ⓔ
B Ⓙ Ⓚ Ⓛ Ⓜ Ⓝ	2 Ⓙ Ⓚ Ⓛ Ⓜ Ⓝ	4 Ⓙ Ⓚ Ⓛ Ⓜ Ⓝ	6 Ⓙ Ⓚ Ⓛ Ⓜ Ⓝ	8 Ⓙ Ⓚ Ⓛ Ⓜ Ⓝ	10 Ⓙ Ⓚ Ⓛ Ⓜ Ⓝ

TEST 4   CAPITALIZATION

A Ⓐ Ⓑ Ⓒ Ⓓ	1 Ⓐ Ⓑ Ⓒ Ⓓ	3 Ⓐ Ⓑ Ⓒ Ⓓ	5 Ⓐ Ⓑ Ⓒ Ⓓ	7 Ⓐ Ⓑ Ⓒ Ⓓ	9 Ⓐ Ⓑ Ⓒ Ⓓ
B Ⓙ Ⓚ Ⓛ Ⓜ	2 Ⓙ Ⓚ Ⓛ Ⓜ	4 Ⓙ Ⓚ Ⓛ Ⓜ	6 Ⓙ Ⓚ Ⓛ Ⓜ	8 Ⓙ Ⓚ Ⓛ Ⓜ	10 Ⓙ Ⓚ Ⓛ Ⓜ

TEST 5   PUNCTUATION

A Ⓐ Ⓑ Ⓒ Ⓓ	1 Ⓐ Ⓑ Ⓒ Ⓓ	3 Ⓐ Ⓑ Ⓒ Ⓓ	5 Ⓐ Ⓑ Ⓒ Ⓓ	7 Ⓐ Ⓑ Ⓒ Ⓓ	9 Ⓐ Ⓑ Ⓒ Ⓓ
B Ⓙ Ⓚ Ⓛ Ⓜ	2 Ⓙ Ⓚ Ⓛ Ⓜ	4 Ⓙ Ⓚ Ⓛ Ⓜ	6 Ⓙ Ⓚ Ⓛ Ⓜ	8 Ⓙ Ⓚ Ⓛ Ⓜ	10 Ⓙ Ⓚ Ⓛ Ⓜ

TEST 6   USAGE AND EXPRESSION
Part 1   Usage

A Ⓐ Ⓑ Ⓒ Ⓓ	1 Ⓐ Ⓑ Ⓒ Ⓓ	3 Ⓐ Ⓑ Ⓒ Ⓓ	5 Ⓐ Ⓑ Ⓒ Ⓓ	7 Ⓐ Ⓑ Ⓒ Ⓓ	9 Ⓐ Ⓑ Ⓒ Ⓓ
B Ⓙ Ⓚ Ⓛ Ⓜ	2 Ⓙ Ⓚ Ⓛ Ⓜ	4 Ⓙ Ⓚ Ⓛ Ⓜ	6 Ⓙ Ⓚ Ⓛ Ⓜ	8 Ⓙ Ⓚ Ⓛ Ⓜ	10 Ⓙ Ⓚ Ⓛ Ⓜ

Part 2   Expression

A Ⓐ Ⓑ Ⓒ Ⓓ	12 Ⓙ Ⓚ Ⓛ Ⓜ	15 Ⓐ Ⓑ Ⓒ Ⓓ	18 Ⓙ Ⓚ Ⓛ Ⓜ	21 Ⓐ Ⓑ Ⓒ Ⓓ	24 Ⓙ Ⓚ Ⓛ Ⓜ
B Ⓙ Ⓚ Ⓛ Ⓜ	13 Ⓐ Ⓑ Ⓒ Ⓓ	16 Ⓙ Ⓚ Ⓛ Ⓜ	19 Ⓐ Ⓑ Ⓒ Ⓓ	22 Ⓙ Ⓚ Ⓛ Ⓜ	
11 Ⓐ Ⓑ Ⓒ Ⓓ	14 Ⓙ Ⓚ Ⓛ Ⓜ	17 Ⓐ Ⓑ Ⓒ Ⓓ	20 Ⓙ Ⓚ Ⓛ Ⓜ	23 Ⓐ Ⓑ Ⓒ Ⓓ	

TEST 7 MATH CONCEPTS AND ESTIMATION
Part 1 Math Concepts

A Ⓐ Ⓑ Ⓒ Ⓓ   3 Ⓐ Ⓑ Ⓒ Ⓓ   7 Ⓐ Ⓑ Ⓒ Ⓓ   11 Ⓐ Ⓑ Ⓒ Ⓓ
B Ⓙ Ⓚ Ⓛ Ⓜ   4 Ⓙ Ⓚ Ⓛ Ⓜ   8 Ⓙ Ⓚ Ⓛ Ⓜ   12 Ⓙ Ⓚ Ⓛ Ⓜ
1 Ⓐ Ⓑ Ⓒ Ⓓ   5 Ⓐ Ⓑ Ⓒ Ⓓ   9 Ⓐ Ⓑ Ⓒ Ⓓ   13 Ⓐ Ⓑ Ⓒ Ⓓ
2 Ⓙ Ⓚ Ⓛ Ⓜ   6 Ⓙ Ⓚ Ⓛ Ⓜ   10 Ⓙ Ⓚ Ⓛ Ⓜ

Part 2 Math Estimation

14 Ⓙ Ⓚ Ⓛ Ⓜ   16 Ⓙ Ⓚ Ⓛ Ⓜ   18 Ⓙ Ⓚ Ⓛ Ⓜ   20 Ⓙ Ⓚ Ⓛ Ⓜ   22 Ⓙ Ⓚ Ⓛ Ⓜ   24 Ⓙ Ⓚ Ⓛ Ⓜ
15 Ⓐ Ⓑ Ⓒ Ⓓ   17 Ⓐ Ⓑ Ⓒ Ⓓ   19 Ⓐ Ⓑ Ⓒ Ⓓ   21 Ⓐ Ⓑ Ⓒ Ⓓ   23 Ⓐ Ⓑ Ⓒ Ⓓ   25 Ⓐ Ⓑ Ⓒ Ⓓ

TEST 8 MATH PROBLEM SOLVING AND DATA INTERPRETATION
Part 1 Math Problem Solving

A Ⓐ Ⓑ Ⓒ Ⓓ   1 Ⓐ Ⓑ Ⓒ Ⓓ   3 Ⓐ Ⓑ Ⓒ Ⓓ   5 Ⓐ Ⓑ Ⓒ Ⓓ   7 Ⓐ Ⓑ Ⓒ Ⓓ   9 Ⓐ Ⓑ Ⓒ Ⓓ
            2 Ⓙ Ⓚ Ⓛ Ⓜ   4 Ⓙ Ⓚ Ⓛ Ⓜ   6 Ⓙ Ⓚ Ⓛ Ⓜ   8 Ⓙ Ⓚ Ⓛ Ⓜ   10 Ⓙ Ⓚ Ⓛ Ⓜ

Part 2 Data Interpretation

11 Ⓐ Ⓑ Ⓒ Ⓓ   13 Ⓐ Ⓑ Ⓒ Ⓓ   15 Ⓐ Ⓑ Ⓒ Ⓓ   17 Ⓐ Ⓑ Ⓒ Ⓓ
12 Ⓙ Ⓚ Ⓛ Ⓜ   14 Ⓙ Ⓚ Ⓛ Ⓜ   16 Ⓙ Ⓚ Ⓛ Ⓜ   18 Ⓙ Ⓚ Ⓛ Ⓜ

TEST 9 MATH COMPUTATION

A Ⓐ Ⓑ Ⓒ Ⓓ   1 Ⓐ Ⓑ Ⓒ Ⓓ   4 Ⓙ Ⓚ Ⓛ Ⓜ   7 Ⓐ Ⓑ Ⓒ Ⓓ   10 Ⓙ Ⓚ Ⓛ Ⓜ
B Ⓙ Ⓚ Ⓛ Ⓜ   2 Ⓙ Ⓚ Ⓛ Ⓜ   5 Ⓐ Ⓑ Ⓒ Ⓓ   8 Ⓙ Ⓚ Ⓛ Ⓜ   11 Ⓐ Ⓑ Ⓒ Ⓓ
            3 Ⓐ Ⓑ Ⓒ Ⓓ   6 Ⓙ Ⓚ Ⓛ Ⓜ   9 Ⓐ Ⓑ Ⓒ Ⓓ

TEST 10 MAPS AND DIAGRAMS

A Ⓐ Ⓑ Ⓒ Ⓓ   1 Ⓐ Ⓑ Ⓒ Ⓓ   4 Ⓙ Ⓚ Ⓛ Ⓜ   7 Ⓐ Ⓑ Ⓒ Ⓓ   10 Ⓙ Ⓚ Ⓛ Ⓜ   13 Ⓐ Ⓑ Ⓒ Ⓓ
            2 Ⓙ Ⓚ Ⓛ Ⓜ   5 Ⓐ Ⓑ Ⓒ Ⓓ   8 Ⓙ Ⓚ Ⓛ Ⓜ   11 Ⓐ Ⓑ Ⓒ Ⓓ   14 Ⓙ Ⓚ Ⓛ Ⓜ
            3 Ⓐ Ⓑ Ⓒ Ⓓ   6 Ⓙ Ⓚ Ⓛ Ⓜ   9 Ⓐ Ⓑ Ⓒ Ⓓ   12 Ⓙ Ⓚ Ⓛ Ⓜ   15 Ⓐ Ⓑ Ⓒ Ⓓ

TEST 11 REFERENCE MATERIALS

A Ⓐ Ⓑ Ⓒ Ⓓ   4 Ⓙ Ⓚ Ⓛ Ⓜ   8 Ⓙ Ⓚ Ⓛ Ⓜ   12 Ⓙ Ⓚ Ⓛ Ⓜ   16 Ⓙ Ⓚ Ⓛ Ⓜ   20 Ⓙ Ⓚ Ⓛ Ⓜ
1 Ⓐ Ⓑ Ⓒ Ⓓ   5 Ⓐ Ⓑ Ⓒ Ⓓ   9 Ⓐ Ⓑ Ⓒ Ⓓ   13 Ⓐ Ⓑ Ⓒ Ⓓ   17 Ⓐ Ⓑ Ⓒ Ⓓ
2 Ⓙ Ⓚ Ⓛ Ⓜ   6 Ⓙ Ⓚ Ⓛ Ⓜ   10 Ⓙ Ⓚ Ⓛ Ⓜ   14 Ⓙ Ⓚ Ⓛ Ⓜ   18 Ⓙ Ⓚ Ⓛ Ⓜ
3 Ⓐ Ⓑ Ⓒ Ⓓ   7 Ⓐ Ⓑ Ⓒ Ⓓ   11 Ⓐ Ⓑ Ⓒ Ⓓ   15 Ⓐ Ⓑ Ⓒ Ⓓ   19 Ⓐ Ⓑ Ⓒ Ⓓ

Test Practice

Test 1 **Vocabulary**

Directions: Read the phrase and the answer choices. Choose the answer that means the same as the underlined word.

Sample A A crafty <u>weasel</u>
- A general
- B athlete
- C business person
- D small mammal

Sample B To <u>approve</u> of the choice
- J agree with
- K help to make
- L talk about
- M explain

1 An unusual <u>accent</u>
- A type of car
- B way of speaking
- C style of clothing
- D place of birth

2 To <u>alert</u> the others
- J see
- K splash
- L warn
- M choose

3 A beautiful <u>gem</u>
- A small star
- B plant
- C fish
- D valuable stone

4 To <u>cling</u> to the doll
- J talk
- K move toward
- L hold tightly
- M compare

5 A <u>definite</u> answer
- A mysterious
- B long
- C quick
- D confident

6 To get <u>drenched</u>
- J replaced
- K soaked
- L injured
- M hired

7 <u>Bind</u> the sticks
- A tie together
- B burn
- C collect
- D break into pieces

8 <u>Concerning</u> my school
- J knowing
- K about
- L like
- M except

GO

9 Visit a relative
A kind of doctor
B forest
C museum
D family member

10 To panic at the news
J hurry away
K call friends
L become afraid
M look around

11 A beautiful canyon
A steep valley
B pond
C creek
D rock formation

12 To hobble around
J jump on one leg
K skip
L walk with difficulty
M slouch

13 Sticky fluid
A candy
B liquid
C covering
D paper

14 A puny tree
J strange
K small
L leafy
M twisted

15 The fleeing deer
A brownish
B spotted
C healthy
D escaping

16 To neglect her work
J begin
K continue
L ignore
M describe

17 An enraged animal
A angry
B unknown
C extinct
D odd

18 To glimpse the mountain
J climb with difficulty
K fear
L worship
M see briefly

STOP

Directions: Read the passage and the answer choices. Choose the answer you think is better than the others.

Sample A   Anwar looked at the sailboat coming into the harbor. It was medium sized, but with its sails furled, it looked smaller than it was. He saw several people on the deck but could not pick out which one was his cousin. He and Eliza had been best friends until she had moved away several years ago.

How does Anwar feel about seeing his cousin Eliza?
A   Worried about the boat
B   Eager to see her
C   Angry that she moved
D   Anxious because he can't swim

Because of their size and ferocity, hurricanes may be the most feared storms on earth. A hurricane is a violent tempest that begins at sea. It is made up of strong winds that blow 74 miles-per-hour or more. To be called a hurricane, the storm must start near the equator in the Atlantic or eastern Pacific Oceans.

Hurricanes form above warm, tropical waters when different thunderstorms start to combine. Their storm winds begin to rotate in a circular or spiral motion. These winds are caused by the spinning of the Earth. As the winds continue to spin and combine, they form one huge storm—a hurricane. The eye of the hurricane is usually found in the very center. It is the area that all the wind spins around and is often called "the calm in the storm."

The planet Earth is spinning all the time, and its effect on a hurricane's winds is called the Coriolis force. Because of the Coriolis force, hurricanes are somewhat predictable. They move northwest or southwest, and they can never cross the equator.

Hurricanes can be tracked with satellites. This allows people to prepare for their arrival. Although hurricanes can be very destructive, they do serve an important function. Hurricanes help provide weather control for the whole planet. During a hurricane, massive amounts of warm air are lifted up and moved to the north or south. This helps to prevent the tropical regions of the Earth from getting too hot. It also helps warm the colder areas. Further, hurricanes help bring rainfall to areas of the world that have been dry for too long.

The power of a hurricane is almost unfathomable. One scientist has calculated that if we could take all the heat energy an average hurricane creates in one day and convert it to electricity, the hurricane would provide all the power the United States would need for the next 16 years!

GO

Directions: Use the reading passage on page 89 to answer questions 1–6.

1 **The Coriolus force is caused by**
A the rotation of the Earth.
B a violent tempest that begins at sea.
C hurricanes moving north and southwest.
D the tracking of satellites.

2 **The phrase *the calm in the storm* describes**
J the period after a hurricane.
K the center of a hurricane.
L the period before a hurricane.
M the tropical area where a hurricane
    starts.

3 **How are hurricanes helpful?**
A They are harnessed for electrical power.
B They allow scientists to track satellites.
C They adjust temperature and rainfall.
D They usually happen along the equator.

4 **What is most predictable about hurricanes?**
J When they will strike next
K How destructive they will be
L How long they will last
M What directions they will travel

5 **In the first paragraph, what does the word
ferocity mean?**
A Direction
B Violence
C Where they start
D How they are formed

6 **What seems to be the purpose of the first
half of this article?**
J To warn about the dangers of
    hurricanes
K To tell how fierce hurricanes can be
L To explain how hurricanes form
M To discuss the benefits of hurricanes

GO

Tortoise Canyon was our special place. We named it for the tortoise we found, slowly making its way up the hillside. Lexie had been to the canyon many times before with Grandfather and had seen salamanders, dragonflies, deer, skunk, and even bobcats—but never a tortoise. "In honor of my kid brother's first visit," she said, "I hereby proclaim this Tortoise Canyon!"

So began our regular travels through the riches that lay on the other side of the winding country road behind our house. Stepping into Tortoise Canyon was like entering another world. The sound of water spilling from a waterfall into the creek below erased all sound. The air was cooler and the plants more lush. New ferns uncurled their fuzzy arms, reaching for sunlight. Tree roots formed sitting perches, and stones were wrapped in luxurious green moss.

We dreamed, planned, and pretended there. Lexie performed original plays with me as her adoring audience. A crown of leaves transformed her into Queen Nefertiti. We finishing each visit with a few moments at the top of the waterfall. There we would sit, dangling our feet into the water, tossing stones into the creek below.

When Lexie went away, I felt like I had lost my best friend. "Even an actress needs an education," she explained, promising to come home soon. The four years she was gone seemed like an eternity.

At last, my long-lost sister was returning! Now that she had her education, she would never have to leave again. Best of all, she had a surprise. But Lexie's surprise turned out to be a young man named Phillip. Phillip had asked Lexie to marry him. Beaming proudly, Lexie introduced her husband-to-be to the whole family.

Lexie and I took a walk through Tortoise Canyon that afternoon. We went straight to the top of the waterfall to sit in our favorite spot. "I'll sure miss being here with you," Lexie said with a heavy sigh. "I'll have to rely on this," she said, tapping her head.

She was right. We had exercised our imaginations together for years. Now we would have to keep alive the memories of those times. Vowing to remember Tortoise Canyon, each of us tossed a stone over the cascading falls. Far below, a pair of ripples expanded across the surface of the water. As we left our secret place, I thought of what would come. I imagined a skydiver leaping from a plane into the endless sky.

7 **Who first introduced the boy to Tortoise Canyon?**
A   His sister's friend
B   His grandfather
C   His next door neighbor
D   His older sister

8 **What does the boy imagine about his sister?**
J   She will become a famous movie star.
K   She has finally come home to stay.
L   She has forgotten about Tortoise Canyon.
M   She will take him on a trip someday.

9 **Where has the boy's sister been?**
A   No one knows
B   Learning how to be an actress
C   Away at college
D   With her Grandfather

GO

10 How does the sister feel about leaving her family for good?

J　She is nervous.

K　She is relieved.

L　She is sad but excited.

M　She is filled with guilt.

11 Why do the boy and his sister throw stones over the waterfall at the end of the story?

A　To see whose stone will make the most ripples

B　To pass time while they talk about the past

C　To express their closeness and their hopes

D　To see if it the pool below is shallow or deep

12 In the last paragraph, the mention of a skydiver leaping from a plane helps to emphasize

J　the extreme height of the waterfall.

K　the wind that rustled through the canyon.

L　the sister's love of doing dangerous things.

M　the boy's thoughts about the future.

13 A walk through Tortoise Canyon would be most like a

A　mystery story.

B　delicious meal.

C　treasure hunt.

D　funny movie.

GO

Skunk

Daylight sees me wander not,
in an earthen den I hide.
At night I scavenge yonder lot,
with moonlight as my guide.

Crickets, beetles, other bugs—
all of them are tasty.
I nibble at my midnight snacks,
trying not to be too hasty.

No man, no beast will be my friend.
It's true, there's little cause.
If suddenly approached or threatened,
I bother not to pause.

I swiftly spray my stinky stench,
my fragrant, foul perfume.
It fills the air, it makes them run.
Must they always leave so soon?

14 When does the skunk feed?
J   Just after sunrise
K   Late morning
L   Just before sunset
M   Late at night

15 Why is the moonlight called a guide?
A   It tells the skunk what time it is.
B   It helps the skunk find things.
C   It leads the skunk to safety.
D   It makes the skunk feel less lonely.

16 In the line about how the skunk frightens everyone away, the poet uses words that
J   rhyme with the word spray.
K   have more than one meaning.
L   begin with the same letter.
M   make the skunk seem human.

17 The words "Daylight sees me wander not, in an earthen den I hide" tell the reader that skunks
A   sleep during the day.
B   are afraid of the sun.
C   disguise themselves with dirt.
D   do not leave their homes.

STOP

Directions: Fill in the space for any word that has a spelling mistake. If there is no mistake, fill in the last answer space.

Sample A			Sample B		
	A	blamed		J	fowntain
	B	hungery		K	pronounce
	C	obtain		L	magazine
	D	collecting		M	shower
	E	(No mistakes)		N	(No mistakes)

1
A arrangements
B whiskers
C borroes
D swampy
E (No mistakes)

2
J umbrella
K enemies
L rowboat
M jingkle
N (No mistakes)

3
A human
B stadeum
C ordering
D bottom
E (No mistakes)

4
J pardon
K natureal
L salty
M citizen
N (No mistakes)

5
A flavor
B praise
C alligator
D several
E (No mistakes)

6
J manner
K warmth
L strenth
M attend
N (No mistakes)

7
A partner
B breathe
C immediately
D puddel
E (No mistakes)

8
J telefone
K unfair
L envelope
M pier
N (No mistakes)

9
A location
B second
C desertted
D plump
E (No mistakes)

10
J fireplace
K voyage
L actor
M seasions
N (No mistakes)

STOP

Test Practice

Test 4 **Capitalization**

Directions: Fill in the space for the answer that has a mistake in capitalization. Fill in the last answer space if there is no mistake.

Sample A	A B C D	President Taft's ancestors lived in Massachusetts and Vermont but were originally from England. (No mistakes)
Sample B	J K L M	Erik Gustafson is looking forward to a week-long trip to Washington with his history class this spring. (No mistakes)

1
A   If you are picky about the fruit
B   you eat, shop at Sheridan's fruits
C   on the east side of the river.
D   (No mistakes)

2
J   Mrs. Dominiqez decided to call
K   an animal rescue service when a
L   Squirrel got trapped in her chimney.
M   (No mistakes)

3
A   Whenever we go camping, Dad
B   and uncle Steve take the boat out
C   to the lake and pretend to catch fish.
D   (No mistakes)

4
J   Route 66 was not the
K   first Highway to be built, but
L   it's certainly the most famous.
M   (No mistakes)

5
A   My father has worked as a
B   travel agent for years. He's been
C   to every country in south America.
D   (No mistakes)

6
J   The best book I ever read was
K   written by C.S. Lewis. It was called
L   The lion, the witch and the wardrobe.
M   (No mistakes)

7
A   On her trip to bali, Marianne
B   bought a beautiful bracelet made
C   of hammered copper and silver.
D   (No mistakes)

8
J   Dad said, "come have a look at
K   the huge crow in our birdbath,
L   and try not to make any noise!"
M   (No mistakes)

9
A   The children's parade started in
B   front of the county courthouse and
C   finished at the park on water street.
D   (No mistakes)

10
J   More photographs are taken
K   of the heceta head lighthouse than
L   of any other in the United States.
M   (No mistakes)

STOP

Directions: Fill in the space for the answer that has a mistake in capitalization. Fill in the last answer space if there is no mistake.

Sample A
- A   Have you ever said something
- B   you felt sorry about afterwards.
- C   It pays to think before you speak.
- D   (No mistakes)

Sample B
- J   The Fitches do their household
- K   chores on Saturday. If they finish by noon,
- L   they go to the hotdog stand.
- M   (No mistakes)

1
- A   "We have tomato sauce cheese,
- B   onions, olives, and pepperoni. What
- C   else goes on a pizza?" Dad asked.
- D   (No mistakes)

2
- J   Dale made sure to invite
- K   Mr. Wilson, his first music teacher,
- L   to the schools spring musical.
- M   (No mistakes)

3
- A   When Lila heard the screech
- B   of the delivery truck's wheels, she
- C   rushed out to greet it's driver.
- D   (No mistakes)

4
- J   Paula smiled at me and said "We
- K   get along well because we like the
- L   same things and think the same way."
- M   (No mistakes)

5
- A   Chef Julia Child cared little for
- B   cooking as a girl She made only mud
- C   pies. Many people find that surprising.
- D   (No mistakes)

6
- J   A great snow had fallen,
- K   so we wrapped ourselves in
- L   woolen mittens, and scarves.
- M   (No mistakes)

7
- A   Renting movies on videotapes
- B   for the family is cheaper than taking
- C   everyone to the movie theater.
- D   (No mistakes)

8
- J   Before she went to the bank,
- K   Carrissa separated and counted the
- L   pennies, nickles, dimes, and, quarters.
- M   (No mistakes)

9
- A   Uncle Gordon loved to laugh. He
- B   thought everyone should laugh more
- C   and that "laughter was the best medicine."
- D   (No mistakes)

10
- J   Many of our favorite folktales are
- K   similar to those from other countries.
- L   Little Red Riding Hood is one example.
- M   (No mistakes)

STOP

Test Practice

Test 6 Part 1 Usage

Directions: Fill in the space for the answer that has a mistake in usage. Fill in the last answer space if there is no mistake.

Sample A	A	If your lucky enough to have
	B	strong enamel on your teeth,
	C	you may not get many cavities.
	D	(No mistakes)

Sample B	J	In the nursery rhyme with
	K	the cat and the fiddle, the dish
	L	had ran away with the spoon.
	M	(No mistakes)

1
A   Danielle wanted to sign up for
B   the trip, but without her own bike,
C   it would might not be as much fun.
D   (No mistakes)

2
J   People who stretch before
K   they go running are less likelier
L   to injure themselves.
M   (No mistakes)

3
A   Carl reached toward the ball
B   and felt it land in his mitt. It was
C   the first fly he ever catch.
D   (No mistakes)

4
J   Dominick likes going to hockey
K   games. His parents buy tickets
L   to a game once or twice a month.
M   (No mistakes)

5
A   After all the leafs had fallen, the
B   children enjoyed raking them into
C   large piles of gold, red, and brown.
D   (No mistakes)

6
J   How do children show signs
K   of wanting independence? They
L   ask to do everything theirselves.
M   (No mistakes)

7
A   My cousin and me look
B   so much alike that many people
C   have asked if we are sisters.
D   (No mistakes)

8
J   Aaron's parents works
K   for the same company, so
L   they often commute together.
M   (No mistakes)

9
A   This rippling creek has been here
B   for as long as I can remember, but
C   that there canal was built last year.
D   (No mistakes)

10
J   Lester Vogel brought a camera
K   on his trip to the Grand Canyon.
L   He used all his film in just a day.
M   (No mistakes)

STOP

Test Practice

Test 6 Part 2 **Expression**

Sample A   Choose the best opening sentence to add to the paragraph below.

A   Grandfather taught Dad to play pool, and Dad taught me.

B   Pool is the most popular billiard game in the United States.

C   Slate is a common material that is used in many different ways.

D   The playing surface of a pool table usually determines its quality.

Sample B   Which sentence should be left out of the paragraph?

J   Sentence 2

K   Sentence 3

L   Sentence 4

M   Sentence 6

Directions: Use this paragraph to answer questions 11–14.

¹A pool table with a surface made of slate is considered to be the best. ²Slate splits naturally and is harvested in large, flat segments about an inch thick. ³Slate is a smooth gray rock that provides a durable playing surface. ⁴Cheaper pool tables are made with materials like particle board. ⁵Since some pool tables feature a single slab of slate, many use three separate slabs. ⁶Getting three slabs to match perfectly, it can be a challenge.

11   Where is the best place for sentence 3?

A   Where it is now

B   Between sentences 1 and 2

C   Between sentences 5 and 6

D   After sentence 6

12   What is the best way to write the underlined part of sentence 5?

J   With some pool tables

K   Unless some pool tables

L   Although some pool tables

M   (No change)

13   What is the best way to write the underlined part of sentence 6?

A   to match perfectly can be

B   to match perfectly, and it can be

C   to match perfectly is being

D   (No change)

14   Choose the best concluding sentence to add to this paragraph.

J   Because the slate is so heavy, it needs four to eight legs to support it.

K   A piece of felt or cloth is stretched over the slate and stapled to the frame.

L   Much of the slate that is used for pool tables comes from Italy.

M   However, smaller slabs travel more easily and are less likely to break.

GO

15
A A large crow taking a dip in our tiny birdbath. I was surprised to see it.

B Taking a dip in our tiny birdbath, I was surprised to see a large crow.

C I was surprised to see a large crow taking a dip in our tiny birdbath.

D In our tiny birdbath, taking a dip, I was surprised to see a large crow.

16
J To make it smell less fishy, tuna salad, when you make it add lemon juice.

K When you make tuna salad, add lemon juice to make it smell less fishy.

L Making it smell less fishy, when you make tuna salad, add lemon juice.

M Add lemon juice when you make it, tuna salad will smell less fishy.

17
A A fresh coat of paint a group of college kids gave our house last summer.

B Last summer, a group of college kids gave our house a fresh coat of paint.

C Giving our house a fresh coat of paint last summer, a group of college kids.

D A group of college kids, they gave it a fresh coat of paint last summer.

18
J We bought Dad a new pair of slippers, but he wears his socks instead.

K Some new ones we bought him, but Dad wears his socks instead.

L We bought a new pair of slippers but Dad, he wears his socks instead.

M A new pair of slippers we bought Dad instead he wears socks.

19 **Which of these would be most appropriate in a thank-you letter to a distant relative?**

A Thanks a lot for the money. Although it wasn't much, every little bit helps. I used it to get a pair of shoes. Because of your money, I didn't have to dip into my savings.

B I'm writing to thank you for the thoughtful birthday card and check. I used the money to help pay for a new pair of running shoes. Thanks to you, I'm ready for cross country this fall.

C Wow, it was really nice of you to send me money for my birthday this year. You never sent anything in the past, so I did not expect to get a card or money! Are you feeling rich?

D Mom and Dad told me I should send you a thank-you note. I spent your money on a pair of shoes that I have wanted for a while. Your money wasn't quite enough though.

GO

Directions: For questions 20–23, choose the best way to write the underlined part of the sentence.

20 I was about to win the game **when** I rolled a double six and landed in jail.

J   since   K   despite   L   because   M   (No change)

21 Because Vera was so curious, she was not afraid **trying** something new.

A   if she tries   B   to try   C   for to try   D   (No change)

22 People who travel to India and **had seen** the Taj Mahal say it is spectacular.

J   saw   K   see   L   will have seen   M   (No change)

23 The lion in *The Wizard of Oz* appeared to be not only cowardly but **shyly.**

A   rather shyful.   B   he was shy, too.   C   shy.   D   (No change)

24 Which of these would be most appropriate as an opening for an essay on how to do something?

J   I'll tell you what tastes good on a hot day—a smoothie, that's what. You can make a strawberry or a banana one, or any other kind you want. With the push of a button, it's done!

L   No one knows who invented the first smoothie. My guess is that it was probably someone who was hungry and bored and had a lot of fruit sitting around. Does that describe you?

K   There's nothing like a cool, refreshing smoothie to ease the heat of summer. To make your own smoothie, all you'll need is a cup of chopped fruit, some milk, ice, and a blender.

M   Smoothies got their name for being what they are—smooth. If smoothies weren't smooth, they'd probably be called crunchies or crispies. No one would drink something with a name like that.

STOP

Test Practice

Test 7 Part 1 **Math Concepts**

Directions: Read each mathematics problems. Choose the answer that is better than the others.

Sample A   What is the value of the 4 in 12.74?

A   4 tenths
B   4 hundredths
C   4 ones
D   4 tens

Sample B   The closest estimate of $7.42 + $2.61 is _____.

J $8
K $9
L $10
M $11

---

1   Which number is between 6,135 and 6,413?

A   6,115
B   6,125
C   6,203
D   6,414

2   Ely read 20 pages in 1 hour and then 10 pages in the next hour. What was Ely's average reading speed for the 2 hours?

J   10 pages per hour
K   15 pages per hour
L   20 pages per hour
M   30 pages per hour

3   What should replace the △ in the multiplication problem on the right?

A   0
B   7
C   8
D   9

```
      4 9 4
  ×    2 2
    ─────────
      9 8 8
    9 △ 8
  ─────────
  1 0 8 6 8
```

4   If the 6 in 7,678 is changed to a 1, how is the value of the number changed?

J   The number increases by 500.
K   The number increases by 600.
L   The number decreases by 500.
M   The number decreases by 600.

5   How many blocks are needed to make the figure below?

A   9
B   18
C   38
D   54

6   Coral's plane leaves at 4:20 P.M. and it is 11:10 A.M. now. How long does Coral have until her plane leaves?

J   7 hours and 10 minutes
K   6 hours and 30 minutes
L   5 hours and 10 minutes
M   5 hours and 20 minutes

GO

7 Reading from left to right, which numerals are represented by the □, △, and ◇ on the number line below?

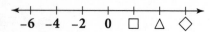

A   2, 4, 6

B   6, 4, 2

C $\frac{1}{6}, \frac{1}{4}, \frac{1}{2}$

D $\frac{1}{2}, \frac{1}{4}, \frac{1}{6}$

8 If the sum of 11 and another whole number is 20, which of the following would best describe both the numbers?

J   Both are odd.

K   Both are even.

L   Both are prime.

M   One is odd and one is even.

9 On a car's speedometer, 1 unit represents 10 miles per hour (mph). If you are going 65 mph, what does the speedometer read?

A   1 unit

B   6.5 units

C   10 units

D   65 units

10 Spinning the shape below could create the illusion of which solid figure?

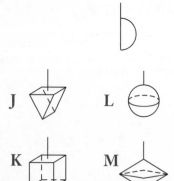

11 Simone has 3 red gumballs, 5 white gumballs, and 2 green gumballs in a jar. If she takes gumballs out of the jar without looking, at most how many gumballs will Simone have to take out of the jar before she is sure to get 2 gumballs of the same color?

A   3

B   4

C   5

D   10

12 Which is the same as six hundred fifty-nine thousand, three hundred twenty-four?

J   659,324

K   60,059,324

L   60,059,000,324

M   600,590,030,024

13 A measurement of 4 meters probably describes the length of a

A   train

B   passenger car

C   skateboard

D   ski

GO

Directions: For each question, choose the answer that is the best estimate of the exact answer.

14 The closest estimate of 38,941 + 10,303 is _____ .
  - J   5,000
  - K   50,000
  - L   500,000
  - M   5,000,000

15 One tennis ball costs 53¢. The closest estimate to the cost of 8 tennis balls is _____ .
  - A $3
  - B $4
  - C $5
  - D $6

16 The closest estimate of $55.96 ÷ 7 is _____ .
  - J $5
  - K $6
  - L $7
  - M $8

17 Jamilyn's bedroom has 148 square feet. Frankie's bedroom has 208 square feet. About how many more square feet does Frankie's bedroom have than Jamilyn's bedroom?
  - A   60 square feet
  - B   70 square feet
  - C   80 square feet
  - D   90 square feet

18 The closest estimate of 531 × 85 is _____ .
  - J   500 × 80
  - K   600 × 80
  - L   600 × 90
  - M   500 × 90

19 A restaurant has 18 waitresses, 9 cooks, and 98 diners. Which best shows how to get the closest estimate of the total number of people in the restaurant?
  - A   10 + 10 + 100
  - B   20 + 0 + 90
  - C   20 + 0 + 100
  - D   20 + 10 + 100

STOP

20 The closest estimate of 493 ÷ 72 is _____ .

J   5
K   6
L   7
M   8

21 Terri walked on stilts for 207 feet. Ross could only walk on stilts for 143 feet. Which is the closest estimate of how much farther Terri walked on stilts than Ross.

A   50 feet
B   100 feet
C   150 feet
D   200 feet

22 The closest estimate of 1243 ÷ 59 is _____ .

J   20
K   200
L   2,000
M   20,000

23 Sarah's mom leaves the house in the morning for work at 6:43 and she arrives at work at 8:12. The closest estimate of how long it takes Sarah's mom to get to work is _____ .

A   1 hour
B   1 hour 30 minutes
C   2 hours
D   2 hours 30 minutes

24 Which best shows how to get the closest estimate of $2\frac{4}{5} + 7\frac{2}{9} + 5\frac{3}{4}$?

J   3 + 7 + 6
K   3 + 7 + 5
L   3 + 8 + 6
M   2 + 7 + 5

25 One square foot of deck costs $7.86 to build. The deck will be 90 square feet. The closest estimate of how much the new deck will cost is _____ .

A $70
B $700
C $7,000
D $70,000

STOP

Test Practice

Test 8 Part 1 **Math Problem Solving**

Directions: Read each mathematics problems. Use the chart below to help choose the answer that is better than the others.

Sample
A   How much more does a toy from Bin 2 cost than a toy from bin 3?
  A   35¢
  B   85¢
  C $1.25
  D   Not given

Directions: The Red Mountain Amusement Park lowered it's for the weekend. The list below shows the items for sale. Use the list to answer questions 1–8.

```
Red Mountain Amusement Park Sale
Toys
  Bin 1           $1.00
  Bin 2           25¢
  Bin 3           60¢
  Bin 4           $1.75
  Balloons        25¢
  Stickers        2 for 7¢, or 5 for 15¢

Food
  Popcorn         10¢
  Soda Pop        30¢, or 3 for 50¢
  Hot Dogs        45¢

Ride Tickets
  Roller coaster  55¢
  Haunted House   30¢
  Ferris wheel    75¢
  Fun House       $1.00

Rentals
  Baby Stroller   $3.40
```

1   T. J. rented 2 baby strollers at the park. How much did he spend?
  A $3.80
  B $5.40
  C $6.80
  D   Not given

2   Celia bought a hot dog, a soda pop, a bag of popcorn, and a ticket to the Ferris wheel. How much did Celia spend?
  J   85¢
  K   95¢
  L $9.50
  M   Not given

3   Eric bought 5 toys from bin 1 and 1 toy from bin 2. Dionne only bought 3 toys, but her total bill was the same as Eric's. From which of the bins could Dionne have gotten her toys?
  A   All 3 toys came from bin 2.
  B   All 3 toys came from bin 4.
  C   Two toys came from bin 1 and one from bin 4.
  D   We cannot tell where Dionne's toys came from.

4   George bought 3 soda pops. How much more did he spend than if he had only bought 1 soda pop?
  J   15¢
  K   20¢
  L   25¢
  M   30¢

GO

5 Hannah spent $1.00 on soda pop and $1.50 on toys. What do you need to know to figure out how many toys she bought.

A She spent $2.50 in all.

B She bought 6 soda pops.

C She bought 1 toy from bin 3.

D All of the toys were from bin 2.

6 Bridget bought 32 tickers. How can she figure out how much she should pay?

J Multiply 11 times 7¢; then multiply 2 times 15¢ and add the results together

K Multiply 6 times 15¢ and add 7¢

L Multiply 16 times 7¢

M Multiply 32 times 7¢

7 Caleb wants to buy a giant giraffe. He thought that he had $21, but he only has $18. The giant giraffe costs $34. How much more money does Caleb need to pay for the giant giraffe?

A $3

B $13

C $16

D Not given

8 Maria has 18 rocks in her collection and twice as many fossils. How many rocks and fossils does she have in all?

J 27

K 36

L 45

M 54

9 For her birthday, Maria received a gift certificate for $25 to the Rocks and Bones Shop. She used the certificate plus $18 to buy two new fossils. One of the fossils cost $22. How much did the other one cost?

A $21

B $23

C $27

D $47

10 Maria arranges her fossils in boxes with a glass top. The boxes are $9\frac{1}{2}$ inches wide. What is the best estimate of how long 6 boxes will be if she puts them side by side?

J 50 inches

K 60 inches

L 70 inches

M 80 inches

STOP

Directions: Use the graph below to answer questions 11–14.

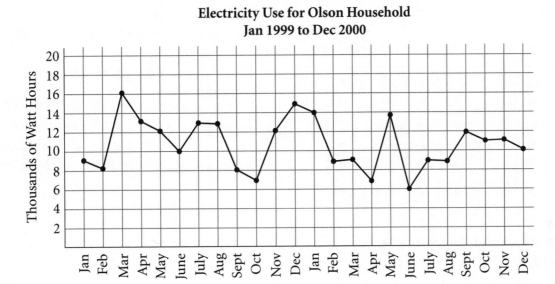

Electricity Use for Olson Household
Jan 1999 to Dec 2000

11 In which month was the electricity usage most nearly the same as the electricity usage in April, 2000?

A March, 2000

B June, 2000

C December, 1999

D October, 1999

12 How many thousands of watt hours are likely to be used by the Olson's in January, 2001?

J Between 1 and 3

K Between 3 and 7

L Between 7 and 14

M Between 14 and 20

13 Which of these best describes the trend of the graph?

A The family seems to be using less electricity over time.

B The family seems to be using more electricity over time.

C The average electric use is increasing quickly.

D There is no way to tell.

14 About how many watt hours did the Olson household use in November, 1999?

J 7,000

K 12,000

L 14,000

M 15,000

GO

Directions: Members of the Prekker family keep a record of their performance in cross country ski races. Below is a table showing their times (T) and the place (P) they finished in races in 1996, 1998 and 2000. The table also shows their ages in 1996. Use the table to answer questions 15–18.

Name	Age	1996		1998		2000	
		T	P	T	P	T	P
Janet	42	18:13	1	19:26	5	17:58	1
Dean	39	19:01	4	19:05	3	18:24	3
Jill	13	23:29	16	21:52	10	19:32	5
Brita	10	28:43	29	24:21	19	21:01	9
Carl	8	30:59	43	27:40	30	24:37	18

15 Whose time dropped the most between 1996 and 2000?
- A   Carl
- B   Brita
- C   Jill
- D   Dean

16 How old was Dean in 2000?
- J   43
- K   41
- L   39
- M   35

17 What is true about Jill, Brita, and Carl?
- A   Their times were about the same.
- B   They all finished in the same place each year.
- C   Their average time was exactly 28 minutes.
- D   Their times decreased each year.

18 In which place did Jill finish the race in 1998?
- J   21
- K   19
- L   10
- M   16

STOP

Test Practice

Unit 10

Test 9 **Math Computation**

Directions: Solve each problem. Choose the answer you think is correct. If the correct answer is not given, fill in the space for the last answer, N.

| **Sample A** $7\overline{)350}$ = | A 45
B 50
C 52
D N | **Sample B** 739 − 57 = | J 692
K 722
L 796
M N |

1

$$\begin{array}{r} 760 \\ -\ 137 \\ \hline \end{array}$$

A 523
B 623
C 630
D N

2 2183 × 3 =

J 2186
K 6633
L 6649
M N

3 5 + 423 + 88 =

A 516
B 606
C 1011
D N

4 0.9 − 0.3 =

J 0.06
K 0.6
L 6
M N

5 800 ÷ 50 =

A 16
B 40
C 850
D N

6 5.7 + 0.8 =

J 5.15
K 6.5
L 13.7
M N

7 $16\overline{)227}$

A 11 R1
B 14
C 14 R3
D N

8

$$\begin{array}{r} \frac{7}{8} \\ -\ \frac{5}{8} \\ \hline \end{array}$$

J $\frac{1}{8}$
K $\frac{1}{4}$
L $1\frac{1}{4}$
M N

9

$$\begin{array}{r} 7496 \\ +\ 4866 \\ \hline \end{array}$$

A 11,350
B 11,362
C 12,362
D N

10 5.09 + 0.38 =

J 4.71
K 6.29
L 547
M N

11

$$\begin{array}{r} \frac{4}{9} \\ +\ \frac{2}{9} \\ \hline \end{array}$$

A $\frac{6}{81}$
B $\frac{6}{18}$
C $\frac{2}{3}$
D N

STOP

Directions: Read the directions for each section. Choose the answer that you think is better than the others.

Sample A

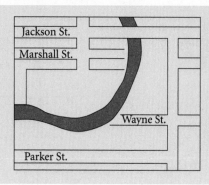

Which street appears to have a bridge across the river?

A   Parker St.
B   Jackson St.
C   Marshall St.
D   Wayne St.

Directions: A summer crafts class used these diagrams to make a book cover out of wallpaper and cardboard scraps. The numbers shown are in inches. Use the diagrams to answer questions 1–4.

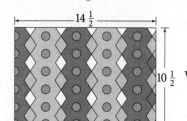

Wallpaper

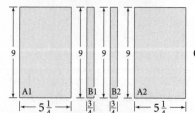

Cardboard

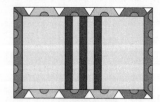

Inside cover, partially assembled

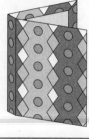

Stapled spine

1   What part of the book cover are parts B1 and B2?

A   The front
B   The back
C   The inside spine
D   The outside spine

2   When the cover is folded and the spine is stapled together, which piece cannot be seen from the inside?

J   Piece W
K   Piece A1
L   Piece A2
M   Piece B1

3   When the pieces are assembled, which two pieces are not touching each other?

A   Pieces W and A1
B   Pieces W and A2
C   Pieces B1 and B2
D   Pieces W and B1

4   Which of these is the smallest piece of cardboard from which both pieces A1 and A2 could be made?

J   6" × 11"
K   10" × 11"
L   11" × 18
M   12" × 18"

GO

Directions: A group of produce farms allows visitors to pick their own produce. The farmers got together and created this map and chart. Use the map to answer questions 5–9.

"U-Pick" Fruit & Vegetable Farm

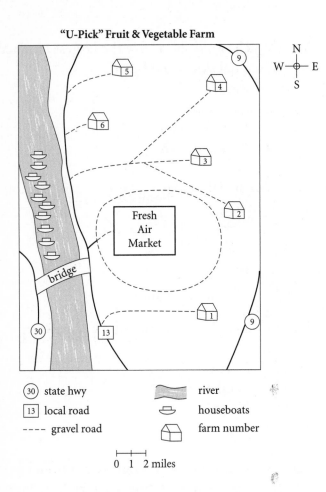

30	state hwy		river
13	local road		houseboats
----	gravel road		farm number

0 1 2 miles

Produce Schedule

	Farm	Hours	Months
Strawberries Raspberries	1	8–3	May–July June–July
Blueberries	2	9–5	July–August
Onions Tomatoes	3	7–6	April–June July–Sept
Squash Pumpkins	4	9–3	July–Sept Sept–Nov
Lettuce	5	8–5	Feb–June
Melon	6	7–8	Aug–Sept

5 During which month would you find the widest variety of berries at U-Pick Farms?
A May
B June
C July
D August

6 How many miles from the bridge is the farm with the longest hours?
J About 5
K About 10
L About 15
M About 20

7 What time could you arrive at U-Pick Farms and find all six farms open?
A Between the hours of 9 and 3
B Between the hours of 8 and 5
C Between the hours of 7 and 3
D Between the hours of 3 and 5

8 What might you find at Fresh-Air Market in July but not in August?
J Squash
K Tomatoes
L Strawberries
M Blueberries

9 The entire western boundary of the U-Pick Farms' property is adjacent to what?
A A state highway
B A gravel road
C A covered bridge
D A river community

GO

Directions: The maps below show a make-believe series of neighboring ski resorts. There are 5 resorts. The top map shows the main lodges, ski runs, and lifts. The bottom map shows the level of difficulty of the areas and the annual number of skiers. Use these maps to answer questions 10–15.

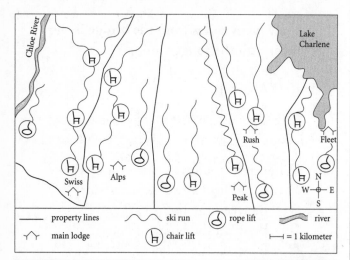

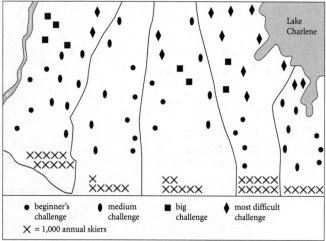

10 To which of the resorts do the most experienced skiers probably go?

J   Rush
K   Fleet
L   Peak
M   Alps

11 Which resort is bordered by a river?

A   Fleet
B   Rush
C   Alps
D   Swiss

12 Which two resorts have the largest number of annual skiers combined?

J   Swiss and Fleet
K   Alps and Peak
L   Peak and Rush
M   Alps and Swiss

13 Which main lodge is southwest of the Alps main lodge?

A   Swiss
B   Peak
C   Rush
D   Fleet

14 In which direction does the Chloe River run?

J   Northwest
K   Southwest
L   Northeast
M   Southeast

15 About how many kilometers is it from the Swiss main lodge to the Rush main lodge?

A   5
B   10
C   15
D   20

STOP

Test Practice

Test 11 **Reference Materials**

Directions: Choose the answer you think is better than the others.

Sample
A

pending	•	penny	631
penpoint	•	pentstemon	632
penultimate	•	percale	633
perceive	•	peregrine	634

On which page would you find the word penguin?

A   631
C   633
B   632
D   634

Directions: Questions 1–7 are about library materials. Choose the best answer for each question.

1 Which of these would contain a list of the planets in the universe?

A   A collection of maps
B   A weather book
C   A space science book
D   A science fiction book

2 Which of these would tell you the meaning of the word pontificate?

J   An almanac
K   A dictionary
L   An encyclopedia
M   A science book

3 Which of these would tell you when Antarctica was first explored?

A   A dictionary
B   A science book
C   A geography book
D   An encyclopedia

4 Which of these would tell you what countries are in the continent of South America?

J   A map of the United States
K   A dictionary
L   A world atlas
M   A book about the South

5 Which of these magazines would most likely have an article about how to repair broken automatic windows?

A   Old Cars Weekly
B   Inside Automotives
C   The Trucker
D   New England Mechanic

6 In which section of the library would you find an encyclopedia?

J   Literature
K   Reference
L   Geography
M   Periodicals

7 Which of these would you find in the index of a book about presidents of the United States?

A   A list the chapters and what pages they begin on.
B   An alphabetical list of words and their definitions.
C   A list of pages with information about Abraham Lincoln.
D   The titles of other books about United States presidents.

Directions: Use this entry from a dictionary page to answer questions 8–14.

---

gim • mick (**gim'** ik), n. a clever device or scheme designed to attract attention or increase appeal.

gla • cial (**glā'** shel), adj. 1. having to do with glaciers or ice sheets. 2. moving extremely slowly.

gos • sa • mer (**gos'** ə mə) n. 1. a fine, filmy cobweb. 2. a thin, light fabric.

goth • ic (**goth'** ik), adj. a style of architecture originating in France in the mid 12th century.

gou • lash (**gōo'** läsh), n. also called Hungarian goulash. a stew of beef or veal and vegetables.

gour • mand (gŏor' **mänd'**, gŏor' mənd), n. a person who is fond of eating.

grack • le (grak'əl), n. a black, long-tailed American bird.

grade (grād), n. 1. a degree or step in advancement. 2. having to do with the slope of a surface such as a road.

grail (grāl), n. a cup or chalice that in medieval legend was associated with unusual powers.

grim • ace (**grim'**əs, gri **mis'**), n. a facial expression that indicates disapproval or pain.

gulch (gulch), n. narrow ravine, often marking the course of a stream.

gul • li • ble (**gul'**ə bəl), adj. easily deceived; trusting.

Pronunciation Guide for this dictionary:

a **rat**	i **bit**	u **nut**	ə stands for
ā **lay**	ī **tie**	û **burn**	a in met**a**l
ä **calm**	ǒ **not**	ŏŏ **look**	o in lem**o**n
ě **net**	o **so**	ōō **root**	
e **me**			

---

8 **How do the two pronunciations of** *gourmand* **differ?**
J   The *g* is pronounced differently.
K   The *ou* is pronounced differently.
L   The *r* is silent in one and not the other.
M   The accent is on different syllables.

9 **What is the plural of gulch?**
A   Gulches
B   Gulchs
C   Gulchies
D   Gulchses

10 **What word best completes the sentence: I never should have believed what the advertisement said; I was far too _____ .**
J   gothic
K   gullible
L   glacial
M   gimmicky

11 **In which sentence is the second meaning of the word glacial used correctly?**
A   From our ship we could see the glacial landscape.
B   My fingers were glacial so I put on some gloves.
C   The line in front of the restaurant moved at a glacial pace.
D   It was nice and glacial outside, so we decided to go skiing.

12 **Which word would best describe a disgusted look?**
J   Goulash
K   Grackle
L   Grail
M   Grimace

Directions: At the top of each page in a dictionary, there are two guide words. They are the first and last words on that page of the dictionary. Use the guide words and page numbers below to answer questions 13–17.

abduction • abstract	25
abstraction • abundance	26
abundant • accumulate	27
accuracy • aerogram	28
aesthetic • affection	29

13 On which page would you find the word **affable**?

A 26
B 27
C 28
D 29

14 On which page would you find the word **abubble**?

J 25
K 26
L 27
M 28

15 On which page would you find the word **acacia**?

A 25
B 26
C 27
D 28

16 On which page would you find the word **adagio**?

J 25
K 26
L 27
M 28

17 On which page would you find the word **accentuate**?

A 25
B 26
C 27
D 28

Directions: Before you use certain reference materials you need to decide exactly which word or phrase to use to find the information you want. We call this word or phrase the key term. In questions 18–20, select the best key term.

18 Which key term should you use to find information about Alice Coachman, an American gold medalist in the Olympic Games.

J Coachman, Alice
K Olympic Games
L gold medalist
M American women

19 Which key term should you use to find out how plants convert light energy into chemical energy to create food for itself in a process called photosynthesis?

A Plants
B Light energy
C Chemical energy
D Photosynthesis

20 The potato is the world's most widely farmed vegetable, and there are hundreds of varieties. Which key term should you use to find a photograph of a Cobbler potato?

J Cobbler potato
K Farming
L Vegetables
M Varieties of vegetables